STREET
TRENDS

STREET TRENDS

How Today's Alternative
Youth Cultures Are Creating
Tomorrow's Mainstream Markets

JANINE LOPIANO-MISDOM AND JOANNE DE LUCA

HarperBusiness
A Division of HarperCollins*Publishers*

A hardcover edition of this book was published in 1997 by HarperBusiness, a division of HarperCollins Publishers.

HarperCollins books may be purchased for educational, business, or sales promotional use. For information please write: Special Markets Department, Harper-Collins Publishers, Inc., 10 East 53rd Street, New York, NY 10022.

First paperback edition published 1998.

Designed by Jenny W. Ng / Sputnik, Inc.

The Library of Congress has catalogued the hardcover edition as follows:

Lopiano-Misdom, Janine, 1960–
    Street trends : how today's alternative youth cultures are creating tomorrow's mainstream markets / Janine Lopiano-Misdom and Joanna De Luca.
      p. cm.
    Includes index.
    ISBN 0-88730-875-9
    1. Youth—United States—Social conditions.   2. Popular culture—United States.   3. Culture.   I. De Luca, Joanne, 1959– .   II. Title.
HQ796.L67   1997
306'.0973—dc21   97-22786

ISBN 0-88730-929-1 (pbk.)

    01 02 ❖/RRD 10 9 8 7 6 5 4 3

Sputnik is a network, a network of individuals who believe passionately in what they do and respect the streets they cover. There wouldn't be a Sputnik without Lisa ("The Big L"), Jenny ("Super Art Director"), Claire, Victor, Walter, Rachel, Amy, Michelle, Anna, Frederic, Kim, Art, Angela, Louise, Warren, Robin, Regina, Sushi, Lucky, Constance, Cameron, Kathy, Ruth, Michele, Thomas P. and S. T. Anthony. And our believers: Stephen, Joe, Anna, Carmela, Jennifer, Nick, Jean, CJ and Keith. Props to Dave and Adrian at HarperBusiness.

For Mary Ann, whose strength throughout was an inspiration.

Special thanks to Mary McGuinness, senior editor, *Sportswear International,* our street editor who burned the late-night oil providing critical insights and great content.

Contents

PART II: THE MINDTRENDS SHAPING TOMORROW

PROLOGUE

We are living in a world of excess. Access to everything and anything has caused this excess. Whether on-line or unplugged, there is choice to the nth degree.

Look around. In the last few years, society has celebrated all that is "new and improved." Whether it's computers, potato chips, or footwear, the turnover of new products quickly fills the retail shelves and our closets. In fact, owning new and improved products, whether soft goods or hard goods, has been equated with "hipness." But the problem that is arising is that in this age of production and consumption, youth culture is finding it hard to keep up with what is "hip" as "all things hip" rapidly roll off the conveyor belt, and what defines "hip" changes instantly in this decade of unrelenting retro.

Moreover, when it comes to information, to which the Web has given society all the access it could ever need, a feeling of anxiety has usurped the initial "wow" factor. Now add this frustrated feeling to the plethora of niche magazines, cable, TV, indie music, indie movies, need-to-know mainstream and pop explosions—and, ironically, the notion of "choice" becomes equated with "effort." In addition, since there is so much to choose from, living in this age of excess has also made people information addicts; no longer are they content to read or listen to one point of view before they make a choice to buy or believe—they want to search it out, investigate every resource and question the data. Why? *Because they can.*

This movement to question has led youth culture to not only question the relevancy of information, but is currently leading them to question the validity and value of products. To be blunt, the era of seduction with "hip" products is over. Youth culture will no longer be rushing to purchase what is "new" as they stand within today's technological, multiplex supermall society, but instead what is "meaningful." In other words, they'll be looking for products that have "soul."

What do we mean by soul? In the year 2000, the only objects that will survive are those that people relate to mentally, spiritually, and emotionally. Products that are deemed "multidimensional."

The question raised then is this: What objects will youth culture decide have the moral right to enter the next millennium? Welcome to the backlash of the twentieth century. Welcome to Civilization Zero.

INTRODUCTION
THIS THING CALLED TOMORROW

Everything about the future and our tomorrow has been planted, molded and nurtured by what is happening in the present. There are no such things as "futurists"; there are no crystal balls or big secrets to unfold. To get there—to be ready for the big explosion of tomorrow—we just need to look at what is brewing today in the progressive microcultures of the streets—those thinkers and doers who move in individual mind-sets, not the masses. What we consider mainstream—the trends, the fads, the gadgets, the styles, the tastes that become popular—often comes from the visual, sensory, emotional cues of those who are considered "the fringe" or "the underground."

To reach them, you need an "in," an entry into their circle. That's what we do at Sputnik. Armed with a video camera, our nationwide network of young correspondents find those progressive thinkers and doers—young street designers, club promoters, DJs, web developers, filmmakers, electronic musicians—and communicate with them on their level, on their turf. We uncover their belief systems and translate how their thoughts and actions will eventually influence mainstream youth lifestyle.

Why is it important to listen to the progressive street cultures? Because these are the mind-sets—the collective thinkers and influencers—that are behind youth's latest infatuation with digital pets, beverages with floating objects, wash-in glitters and mascara hair colors, electronic music that can't be found on any contemporary radio station—and the list goes on.

Through "Mindtrends," our biannual trend report, we track the movements among these progressive mind-sets and interpret them into actionable opportunities for marketing, new product development, brand management and advertising. With more than twenty-eight years of experience in advertising and youth marketing between us, we recognized a need for businesses to get ahead of the so-called "trend curve" and to anticipate the shift or movement that becomes the next "trend."

The tracking of so-called "trends" and "what's cool" is a hot topic these days, mainly because mainstream businesses have been trying to crack the tastes, preferences and styles of the elusive and fickle youth culture. It's understandable why. With over thirty-six billion dollars of expendable income—and yes, they are spending those dollars—everybody wants a piece of the "cool" spenders. But in actuality it's not about what's cool; it's about seeking those with progressive interests, getting inside their heads and understanding the movements they will affect.

Whatever we choose to call them, subcultures or countercultures have entered the mainstream with an idea, a set of values and often, a challenge to what is. From James Dean in the fifties, flower power in the sixties, punk in the seventies, heavy metal and hip-hop in the eighties to grunge in the nineties, trends emanating from youth culture have had a reverberating effect on our mainstream culture, creating "movements." These movements have influenced impressions that affect our tastes, lifestyles, fashion, music and purchasing decisions.

Society, whether we admit it or not, is seeking that next youthquake—the next great movement to define the millennium. We are anxiously awaiting that rebellious and radical surge from youth culture to fuel our creative thoughts, ideas and products for tomorrow.

But why wait? There are cues and signs pointing the way right now. Look around . . . and listen. This is not only the era of individualism, but it's a rapid, full-speed seduction of the computer age. We, as a society, have voyaged into a realm of the unpredictable; the major youth protests and rallies of yesterday seem to have disappeared, when in reality they have gone underground.

If you take anything away from this book, understand that this youth culture is the most resourceful, intellectual, and creative generation that we have seen in the past fifty years. This generation is a force seeking out their own partnerships, mentors, avenues of capital and platforms for communicating. Tracking their interests through the likes of music, sports and entertainment is passé; combining the human factor of personal interaction with the netted world of computers is now the link to youth interests.

The challenge for marketers as we move closer to the millennium is to sort through the confusion of the rapid flow of ideas, the changing street scenes and the fusion of various cultures. Trying to find the next big idea has become more complex as it gets harder and harder to reach young consumers.

The solution: learn to listen and sift through the excitement and energy of what this young consumer wants. There is always a unifying theme, a consistent point of view that spreads throughout youth cultures. Sputnik gets inside the minds and souls of this largest growing consumer group; *Street Trends* tells you why you need the information to survive the lightning-fast changes taking place in the youth marketplace.

For those of us living in this whirlwind of information, there is no bible on what is right, definite, exact or precise about tomorrow. If we listen, if we filter—and let them show us where to look and how to look—only then will we get beyond the unknown and surf into this thing called tomorrow.

Part I

The Streets

1

THE FRINGE CONNECTION

Trend. Such a small word for all the power behind it. A word, a label that often identifies a movement, infiltrates our closets and invades our daily lives. If you think about it, how and where does a trend start? And who are these people that deem something a "trend"? In one form or another, whether we see them or not, trends can affect our lifestyle and our purchasing decisions, and eventually give us a new outlook. The visible manifestations of trends—the ones you can spot easily on the streets—often start with the youth culture.

Youth culture is defined differently by many experts, the most common terms being created and overexposed by the media.

Take, for example, the age group sixteen to twenty-nine—a hot consumer segment that major corporations from automotive to insurance have been scrambling to capture for the past few years. Why? Because they are a strong force, with more than thirty-six billion dollars of expendable income. This age group has been labeled many things recently—"Generation X" or "Gen X," "The Alternative Generation," "Busters," "Slackers." Although the list keeps growing, the most widely used term to describe sixteen- to twenty-nine-year-olds (and, yes, those ages are debatable) is Generation X or Gen X.

Starting as a book title in 1991, *Generation X* was marketed, hyped and overexposed in the media to create a label for individuals then eighteen to twenty-nine years of age. In the jacket description of Douglas Coupland's *Generation X: Tales for an Accelerated Culture*, we are told that this is a "frighteningly hilarious, voraciously readable salute to the generation born in the late 1950s and 1960s—a camera shy, suspiciously hushed generation known vaguely up to now as *twentysomething*." With its self-created definitions and lingo, *Generation X* portrayed a group of three friends whose personal journey was subjectively (or should we say strategically?) interpreted by the media as restless, confused, distraught and disenchanted. Whatever we think, this novel created a new marketing term for a "generation."

Another misnomer loosely used to describe that "generation" is *Slacker*, which was the title of a 1991 independent film by writer-director Richard Linklater. The film's characters were perceived as "angry, cynical, antiestablishment"—again, as described by the media.

Whatever the source, there still exists today a generational picture of angst, cynicism and antivalues that has plagued sixteen- to twenty-nine-year-olds since 1991. Born from the media and hyped by marketers, the characters of a book and a movie have been crowned the mirror of an entire age group.

But we are now beyond that: *Generation X* chronicled a group "born in the late 1950s and 1960s," which, in 1997, would make them between the ages of twenty-eight and forty—a far cry from the marketing standard segment of eighteen- to twenty-nine-year-olds that it labeled. Debating the age issue or demything the Gen X label still leaves marketers in a quandary. Seven years of Gen X hype and marketers are still asking, Who are these people?

Let's forget about age for a minute. The key to understanding youth culture is to understand mind-sets, the collective thinking or similar beliefs that drive people to think and act the way they do. In the traditional realm of market research, we were taught to segment consumer groups by age or generation, because age has always been a factor in conducting quantitative, qualitative, sociological and psychographic profiles. Our age supposedly explains where our influences are coming from, what our needs and monetary means may be, and how we may be reasoning (or not reasoning) things. According to sociology, we are a product of our environment. But in marketing, we are a product of our age group, one big "generation," labeled and tagged and ready to be targeted. According to the media, twentysomethings are Gen X, cynical, antiestablishment, grungy, angry young slackers. Come on, everybody? Lumping an age group—any age group—and characterizing them as one amorphous blob is the kind of thinking that outdates corporate messages and leaves stagnant brands in the dust . . . especially with the educated youth culture coming down the pike.

THE UNITED STREETS OF DIVERSITY

We've been referring to youth culture as one big group, when actually it is a mix of different mind-sets and cultural influences. It's a subsegment of our society, one that we have all been through at one time in our life. Put yourself back in the day . . . remember the word *cliques*? The "in" crowds? Questioning where you fit in and belong? Youth culture today basically faces similar challenges and peer pressures. Today's cliques are called *crews* and finding an identity starts even younger, pushing the envelope further.

There's so much more information coming at them. Beyond MTV, magazines, zines and web sites, influences and cues come from the "streets," the visible trendsetters who dare to walk to a different beat. The buzz for the past five years, the streets have been dictating and translating what is "hip" or "alternative" in youth culture. Facial and body piercing; dark cosmetics (for guys and girls); Japanimation accessories and toys; alien characters; grunge or "indie" style; the retro sixties and seventies craze in fashion and music; the popularity of alternative sports like skateboarding, in-line skating and BMX biking; the multibillion-dollar music genres of hip-hop and alternative—all are examples of the street's mark on the main-stream.

From the punk and Gothic microcultures to the mainstream showcase of grunge, street cultures edit our style, our music and our new media interests. "Street culture" has become synonymous with fringe, or what we once referred to as coun-terculture. But don't look at them as just one group or another—the streets are many subcultures, constantly sam-pling and borrowing from different mind-sets and influences.

Tripping through the youth time warp, music used to set the style, and you could identify the rockers, punks and techno-heads just from their look and their sound. With music melding faster than a CD spins, and everyone listening and mixing dif-ferent styles, what you have is a new formula for their sense of life. Youth today are all one big sample of diversity. Through the media, technology and society, we've all been exposed to other cultures, other mind-sets. Diversity has taught us to cele-brate our differences and to enjoy the difference of others. Today's youth culture is the most ethnically diverse to date, and it's projected that the nonwhite youth population will grow to become 15.5 percent of the population between the years 1996 and 2006. Take a look at the school system in Jersey City, New Jersey, the nation's most ethnically diverse city. St. Luke High School, the subject of a 1996 memoir by Mark Gerson, *In the Classroom: Dispatches from an Inner-City School That Works*, had 430 students who came from forty-two countries. According to the 1990 census, 31 percent of the nation's sixty-four million children are minorities. It's not a matter of what minorities make up those numbers, it's the exciting experiences this diversity will celebrate—the integration of second languages, new religions and beliefs, ethnic foods and so on. The global village truly comes to your hometown.

The streets are just as diverse, not just in the sense of true ethnic cultures, but in the "societies" who share a collective interest or belief. Many of these collective "societies" or street cultures have emerged over time to become a culture all their own, like the Beats of the fifties or the mods of the sixties. Back then, the mainstream, so engrossed in *Father Knows Best*, called such collective groups "countercultures," perceiving them as outsiders against the norm. Among themselves, the so-called countercultures were a culture all their own—a group of free people who stood for a creative vision and for individual freedom against the close-minded bureaucratic system. The street cultures today are very similar, evolving the vision of the fifties Beats and other countercultures to more diverse interests.

> I believe there really are no cultural differences—I mean, culturally, yeah. But this is a new generation, we're making our own culture and it's universal culture, and it's humanity culture. It's, like, where we as young individuals are headed, and I think where we're headed is independence. It's not about an Asian culture, an African culture, an American culture—it's all about a humanity thing here. We're talking about a real global warming—global warming, get it?
>
> —DOMAINI, TWENTY-FIVE, CREATOR OF TRUE TV,
> SAN DIEGO

These are the individuals coming at us, sampling their way through popular culture, pushing a new digital aesthetic that will change the face of how we see, taste, smell and touch consumer goods. How do we see them coming? And, more important, how do we prepare for the inevitable change they will bring?

The most obvious link to the future is to uncover the trends, the cultural or social movements that are brewing—not what is oversaturated and noticeable everywhere today. If it's visible in your neighborhood or crowding your nearest mall, the learning is over. It's too late. That visible trend in your neighborhood may have started years ago with a subculture, a fringe mindset, and has just now manifested itself in the mainstream—like the pierced eyebrow or nose. But *trend* is just a word unless you know the culture behind it . . . and *why*. Why is it emerging? Who says it is a trend? And what does it mean to me?

There's a difference between a trend that is tracked by surveys and spending patterns and one that is an interpretation of a movement, gathered straight from the source—in the case of today's youth, that source being the progressive street cultures. It's not easy to find these street cultures, or to spend some time getting into their heads. That's why we formed Sputnik. We saw a need for businesses to turn to the progressive trendsetters, to get close, to understand what they are doing culturally and socially by tracking the shifts, where they are going or what they will be doing next. These shifts, these movements swell and catch on to become a trend.

Signs of trends that began—or were first made visible—by street cultures are around you today. Take the eighties resurgence—in our clothes, our expensive tastes, our music and our TV reruns. The trend isn't just that the eighties happen to be the retro decade of the moment, but that youth culture was ready to go back to a time when luxury came guilt-free.

The whole theory of why we are susceptible to nostalgia is

Eighties retro hits the streets of New York City in
accessories like the Dionne von Furstenberg sunglasses.
Photo source: "Mindtrends" video report.

that we feel an emotional linkage to a period of time, whether
we lived through it or not. The thrill of going back in time is to
find something *unique*. We're drifting into an eighties nostalgia
because the youth didn't really do the eighties scene—most of
the youth we are talking about were born in the eighties, too
young to join the yuppie race. This youth did the nineties for
us, teaching us how to dress down (via "grunge") and "chill
out." What intrigues youth today about the eighties was all the
"stuff"—how people lavished themselves with quality goods,
designer labels, expensive cars, party-themed nightclubs . . .
well, you get the picture. They had to simplify with all the post-
eighties spenders, now it's their turn. It's not the excessive
spending that's turning them on—it's the search for that unique
experience, for the carefree empowerment the eighties represents.

Sometimes it's not that easy to discover why we are shifting,
or where our youth is moving next. You can't sit back and
expect to watch it on MTV. You need to get down with the
streets, to be in the trenches everyday.

That's what we do at Sputnik. Through our network of young correspondents across the country, we get to the streets, the neighborhoods, the clubs, the basements and the playgrounds, and talk to the street cultures. On their level, their turf—and their time. Our biannual video trend report called "Mindtrends" uncovers and tracks the shifting mind-sets of progressive young street cultures. We then interpret what it will mean to your future, your business. Call it what you want, but predicting a trend means tracking the shifting attitudes of the collective thinkers and doers. This connection to the street cultures is the learning needed to get us on track for a new century—and a new contemporary American culture depersonalized by the media.

VIDEOTAPING THE VIDEO WATCHERS

The networks, cable TV, magazines, newspapers, World Wide Web, et al., are talking at people every day, flashing images telling us what's new, what's hot, what's now. Technology has liberated us, with portable/digital video cameras and satellite linkups. Worldwide news is instantaneous; teenagers in Tokyo know what New York is doing, and vice versa. Marshall McLuhan's vision of the global village has networked beyond connecting cultures and cities—we have created cybercities, transmitting our surreal selves into rooms, interacting with other surreal Netizens (citizens of the Internet, as coined by *Wired* magazine). Via the Internet, we are surrealists who, at the stroke of a key, can create ourselves as the "someone" we always wanted to be, hiding behind the power of the descriptive word. But in a few years, when video conferencing and CU-SeeMe technology invade our home TVs and replace the old chat rooms, we will no longer be able to hide behind the video monitor.

Like corporate marketers who cannot continue to hide

behind one-way focus-group mirrors. That's the old way of gathering information and insights. And how insightful can a focus group be when everyone in the room knows they are being paid to answer questions for a corporation? It's human nature to impress, to sometimes pretend or exaggerate your true self to gain acceptance, especially in a group situation where you feel you are being judged—by others and the people behind the fake mirror. What's lacking is *reality*, the consumer or consumers in their natural environment, relaxed, possibly with their friends, with the interviewer they are having a conversation with—not answering questions and ranking their attitudes on a scale of 1 to 10. Traditionally, focus groups and one-on-one interviews are the closest means to understanding the consumer, by picking individuals representative of the demographic. But who selects these chosen few? Typically, research groups recruit the impersonal way—over the phone or in an exit survey. One phone call and twenty questions later, Ms. Consumer might be the "right" individual who, for a good compensation (average fee: fifty dollars), will answer the question that might save the company. But how do you know they are the "right" ones—have you been in their closets? Trailed their daily routines? Hung out with them socially?

What's lacking is the intimacy, the personal quirks, desires and interests—knowing the individual and the circles of influences around them. Take the example of an athletic footwear manufacturer that wants to enter the alternative sports arena—skateboarding, in-line skating, etc.—because the lifestyle has such a massive impression on youth culture. The key is to be true to the message of the alternative sports culture—use the right words, have the right attitude, music and visuals. To test how "rad" the brand is, they might recruit some teens who fit the consumer profile from the nearest convenience-store parking lot for a focus group. Are they the core consumers, or just the mainstream followers? Think about it—some kid in Minneapolis who has adopted the dress of a skateboarder and has never ollied in his life could be responsible for a multimillion-dollar category launch meant to capture and sell a culture. Scary, huh?

Speaking to the obvious target, a trend follower who hangs on the corner or answers a phone call or participates in a focus group, will only deliver the immediate, the present. What about the future? How does a product or brand image leap ahead of the fickle trend curve? By getting to the trendsetters, the influencers of popular culture.

No, it's not all on MTV anymore. When it first hit the screen, MTV globalized the music of youth culture, spawning a visual style loosely dubbed "MTV-like," a jumpy, quick-cut style of shooting. Anyone under the age of thirty has grown up with this style, accepted it in TV and cinema format as normal. It's the way youth view the world—through a fast-cut, fast-paced camera lens. So what we have today is a generation of fast-paced, media-savvy young video watchers currently creating our home pages and web sites. While we may think that the digital revolution has linked us up, it has also alienated us further from any intimate, one-on-one contact with our consumers.

Enter Sputnik. We get to the grass roots. To the streets. To what people—real people—are saying. What they think ... what their faces and body language reveal. We videotape the video watchers and find out what they like and dislike, their concerns, their desires—and where they are heading next. We get to the individuals who don't do focus groups: the ones creating a new web channel, designing a new line of protective clothing, sampling a new sound in the clubs—the creative individuals influencing others. The trendsetters.

But who deems someone a "trendsetter"? Their peers do, and it's their peers who are the Sputnik correspondents. They are friends of friends; have the same interests, frequent the same places, shop the same stores. The power of finding the trendsetters is to be "in" with them. All of our correspondents at

Sputnik are themselves of the age and mind-set of the people they interview—essentially "one of them"—like Claire, twenty-eight, of Austin, Texas, an independent film producer, writer and Sputnik correspondent who lives and works within Austin's tight independent scene. Or Victor, twenty-five, a designer, patented inventor, and skateboarder residing in New York City.

Rachel and Victor, two of Sputnik's New York
correspondents, uncovering the "why?"

Anyone can enter a "scene," but it's the respect and understanding you have that makes the connection real. Hitting the clubs, the basements, the coffee shops, the schools, the galleries—anyplace that is a haven of street culture—isn't the easy way in. You have to know them. Sputnik gets in through our correspondents who have intimate conversations with progressive individuals and uncover on videotape insights that are deeper than what any magazine or TV show can offer. Often, a correspondent's assignment involves speaking to young individuals to uncover specific concerns for a company, and they have the same interests as the people they need to track. What happens here is magic—the casual, comfortable and honest conversations that reveal a lot of what may never be visible to the naked eye.

Picture this. Vic is at Pacific Drive in San Diego, hanging out with a group of skaters. He takes a turn off a curb and grabs the video camera. A sixteen-year-old kid named Rob sporting a pair of Etnies and a Charles Manson T-shirt does an ollie off the staircase. His friend TJ, who looks no older than twelve, is just sitting on the curb reading the latest *Transworld*. Kate, who hates the tag "Betty" (which refers to any female skater), waits patiently at the rail. Vic asks Kate what she thought of Larry Clark's movie *Kids*. They both know Harold and Akira from the cast, and start talking about the media's lack of respect for the flick. When he asks her about West Coast versus East Coast styles of skating, the others pipe in. Answering genuinely, it is as if they were merely asked for the time. They open up about everything: from rad tricks and the ozone layer to the mass suicide of the cult group Heaven's Gate. And, while puffing away on smokes—legal and nonlegal—they speak directly into the camera and explain the benefits of ginseng-charged drinks and high-protein green vegetables.

Skaters on Pacific Drive in San Diego.
Photo source: "Mindtrends" video report.

Sound confusing? How could someone be concerned about the lack of nutrients in canned goods and the harmful spraying of pesticides on fruits when their favorite shot is Jägermeister and they own a Barney Rubble–shaped water bong? And how does this ever correlate to a "trend"?

The first thing to understand is that this youth culture has a bipolar personality. As humans, we all have a bipolar brain— one side that feeds our creativity, one side that drives our reason. Our likes, dislikes, desires and motivations are all driven by these bipolar forces—what we consider *raw intellect*. We're never one thing; we're a mixed bag of images, going back and forth between the complex and the simple, the future and the past, memory and reality.

This generation—not just the group of skaters that we used as an example—is a generation that is bipolar in personality. This means that youth culture is no longer programmed to believe in one voice or become reliant on one message. They absorb everything and anything they choose, mainly because there is so much out there to choose from. So, like being involved in an experiment, they taste this and that, decide they like it or not, try something else, and so on and so forth. It has nothing to do with the realities of what is good or bad (that comes after the fact), it's about reaching a heightened level. *It's all about the experience.*

No doubt, personalities have always shown that people act out conflicting behaviors. For instance, take the free-thinking sixties hippie culture—there were vegetarianism and natural herbal remedies as well as weed and LSD. What is happening today is an evolution of this progressive-thinking sixties counterculture. Today's street cultures are also embracing holistic habits with decadence as evidenced by their obvious rush to experience the next vibe, sensation, reality or emotion—but it's not considered rebellious or radical, it's considered *okay*.

In today's street culture, you wouldn't consider people to be full-fledged hypocrites if they exhibited obvious contradictions in their behavior. First, if anything, you ask *why*, so that you too can understand what drove them—and yourself—to formulate those opinions. But *why* is it suddenly *okay* to *refuse* to follow one belief system, hold a solid political stance or choose not to adapt to one specific lifestyle? Basically because no one today is in the position to judge. Their peers, as well as our contemporaries, are also searching and surfing the Net for newfound ideologies and perceptions. The majority of youth today are what we call "free radicals," living in the age of information, swiftly absorbing and learning about any point of view that they happen to run into. With the spread of technology—especially personalized, hands-on accessibility—this generation is literally in control. If they want to they can *easily* find out about sadomasochism, serial killers, metaphysical poetry or the life story of Aleister Crowley. Or for that matter, gardening, biotechnology and cybergenics. All that information is there on the World Wide Web, and depending on that person's mood on a particular day, who knows where they will wind up?

Although many would compare the surge of inquisitiveness in today's youth culture to other generations of the past, no one can argue that there has ever before been an era where the power and the freedom to access information created such an explosion. Pandora's box has been opened, and in case we haven't realized, there is virtually nothing to seal it. Just the power of the Internet alone has fueled an appetite for more newness, more experimentation, more information, more discovery.

This, among other things, is what we track at Sputnik. From the hundreds of hours of videotaped interviews from across the country, London and Tokyo, we track the similarities, identify the recurring thoughts or themes and interpret them for major corporations, manufacturers of food, beverages, fashion, cosmetics, shoes and accessories. With fourteen years each of marketing and advertising experience (and a lot of social instinct), we interpret this information as it relates to product development, marketing strategies and consumer communications, all with respect to the consumers the companies target. Not every trend will be embraced in its purest form by the mainstream consumer. The trick is knowing in what form it will filter up to the mainstream.

Through our "Mindtrends" report, Sputnik reveals what the fringe street cultures are doing, and how to interpret it for market and understand how consumers will use it. We illustrate the diversity in their thinking and interests, identified as individual mind-sets: the Collective Intellect, the Soldiers for Culture, the Hip-Hop Nation, the Speed Generation and the Club Kids—and discuss them in chapter 3. But for now, understand that these mind-sets exist everywhere in major urban areas that have strong cultural scenes, art scenes and emerging music scenes, and are often home to a major university or college. Cities like Atlanta, with its strong emerging hip-hop, R&B and alternative music scene; Austin, the home of independent filmmakers and writers and the new hot tech bed; San Diego, where alternative speed sports clash with the alternative music front; and New York City, with its nocturnal club scene, international jet-setting DJs and Lower East Side fashion tribes. Cities that breed individuality by means of their sheer size and density. These are the cities where the young street cultures thrive, and from where their progressive thinking filters out to the early adopters.

2

THE BUBBLE-UP THEORY

Everyone is looking at the streets these days, from couture fashion designers to record producers. And they should—the streets are where to find the true creative visionaries. We went through a period when fashion designers would dictate what was the fashion trend of the moment, but that's changed. The difference is that the young street cultures are now dictating the trends, as their style, their attitude and their tastes bubble up to the likes of producers of fashion, food, beverages, music and movies who need to know "what's next."

Why all the new-found faith in these young street cultures? America is obsessed with youth—with the alpha hydroxides that help us look young, the New Age books that spiritually help us think young and our acceptance of casual Fridays and "dress down days."

In the nineties, we've had our share of noticeable youth-oriented trends—and products addressing a trend: body and facial piercing; retro music; retro clothing (we seem to visit a new decade every three years); retro furnishings; ginseng-charged candy, drinks, gum and cigarettes; beverages with floating edible objects to delight the child in all of us; micro-brew beers; and electronica music like techno, jungle, trip-hop, techtronic, electro and ambient that pulsate the trendiest dance clubs from New York to Los Angeles.

The trend in electronic music is a good example of what was originally considered a street or local "thing" and how it has caught on or "bubbled up" from the clubs. Usually mixed by a DJ using a synthesizer and turntables, techno music has filtered into TV commercials and cartoon themes. Soon most music will be mixed and synthetically created, as technology brings us to new dimensions that man can't mimic with traditional instruments. Look at the synthesizer as the new electric guitar (and we all know how that changed rock and roll forever).

When it first hit the scene, many people didn't think techno music would last. But, like a lot of underground trends, it was born out of a culture. Look at so-called "alternative" rock, rap, hip-hop, disco and metal—they all blew up from the local clubs to the mainstream. A good example of something that started in a subculture and bubbled up to mainstream is the Seattle scene that is credited for "outing" alternative rock and influencing a street style labeled "grunge." Grunge became the fashion rage of the early nineties, and major designers like Donna Karan and Versace introduced their own version of grunge on the runways.

But they missed the big picture here. It's important to look at

The grunge look popular on the streets in the early nineties.
Photo source: "Mindtrends" video report.

the evolution of this thing called grunge to understand how a trend bubbles up from the fringe street cultures to mainstream America. Grunge didn't just materialize as a fashion trend when the media glamorized the Seattle scene. Grunge basically evolved from an ongoing fashion sense that's spanned the youth cultures of the past five decades, starting with the American beatnik poetry scene in the late 1950s.

Jack Kerouac, the godfather of beatniks, didn't wear what's considered the traditional Beat style of black garments, goatee, sandals and beret, which was influenced by the Parisians. Kerouac and his buddy Neal Cassady looked very much like college kids today—crumpled workshirts, sweatshirts, jeans or chinos. Back in the swing skirt, sweater-set and knit-top fifties, this was considered a scruffy antistyle, as chronicled in Kerouac's book *On the Road*. The Kerouac Beat style was to scoff at anything materialistic, an extension of his nomadic, "just passing through" attitude.

From the laid-back style of the original Beats, this same "just passing through" mind-set evolved into the rockers and hippies of the sixties, whose style was as eclectic and psychedelic as you can get. Anyone with long hair, headbands, patched bell-bottom jeans, psychedelic T-shirts and crumpled tops was labeled a "hippie."

Then, in the early nineties, after all the construction boots, Dr. Martens boots, workshirts and baggy jeans, the fringe youth transformed into new "hippie" looks, based on the music they were into—indie kids, riot grrrls, grunge and even ravers. Of all the looks, grunge bubbled up to become mainstream, mainly because of the casual, eclectic mix of style that others considered "dirty" or "grungy," hence the name.

It's important to track fashion and style when looking at the trendsetting street cultures, because this self-expression is what the mainstream can mimic easily. The mainstream can buy into the look without ever getting into why the style serves as the identity of that street subculture. Face it—the evolution of the original Beats to grunge to the eclectic street style of today is an expression of youth—that freer, more experimental time of life. To Kerouac and company, the origins of their laid-back antistyle is that they didn't care about their exterior "selves"—it was insignificant to their verbal expression of individual freedom and intellectual revolution against the bureaucratic system.

Unlike the Beats, today's mainstream youth embrace the expression of individuality in their exterior style, where they can have the most fun and make the most shocking statement showing "who they are." The "bubbling up" of body and facial piercing, riveted, spiked and brightly dyed hair and dark, bloody cosmetic colors are all exterior self-expressions of their individuality.

You can trace the origins of body and facial piercing back thousands of years in other cultures; it is a common tribal rite of passage for sexuality and spirituality. Body and facial piercing is also a rite of passage in the underground fringe cultures, mainly in the sadomasochistic, punk and heavy metal worlds where some body piercing is said to enhance sexual pleasure. So why do the mainstream youth today pierce other parts besides the ear? The body is the one thing they own and can alter. And to a lot of today's youth, piercing is part of "looking good."

(What's it for you in terms of a look?) "Not really grunge, but body piercing, tattoo, short hair . . . very important for your reputation. You have to look good when you're walking down the street. You can't look like an idiot—can't look all dirty and grungy—it ain't good."

—JENNIFER, SEVENTEEN, LOS ANGELES

Jennifer, L.A., on her view of "clean." *Photo source: "Mindtrends" video report.*

No, Jennifer's not an S&M kid, she's a junior in high school who loves to hang out with her friends, dance at "underground" parties, go clubbing with her fake ID. Sounds normal. Jennifer is what you would consider an "influencer"—an early adopter of what the fringe street cultures are doing. She probably learned four years ago to pierce her eyebrow and nose from the people she admired at the clubs. *Whatever.* Today for Jennifer and her generation, body piercing and short dyed hair is what you would call "looking neat."

And when asked what's the one thing she would want in the whole world? "Lots of money so I can pierce my body more—I want to pierce my tongue and lip" (to match her brow and nose).

If you think that you don't see every teenage kid walking the malls with a pierced nose or eyebrow now, then look at how popular earrings have become with guys. Less than fifteen years ago, if you were a guy, you had to be selective of what ear you had pierced—depending on the area, the right or left ear signaled that you were gay. Not true anymore—it's typical for guys to wear an earring. Even sports superstars—male icons like Michael Jordan and Dieon Sanders, who has both ears pierced—wear earrings.

Freestyle sports, a.k.a "extreme" sports, are another example of what the streets have been doing and how they have infiltrated the mainstream. Born from a tight youth miniculture, the "extreme" explosion progressed into the limelight and our TV sets in the mid-nineties. Extreme sports earned their label because the athletes who participate in these sports play outside the bounds of traditional organized sports. Marketers realized that the attitude of these young freestylers was being adopted by mainstream youth, and everything from soft drinks to telephone dialing services to fast food suddenly used the word *extreme* in their marketing messages. But they missed the point—these so-called sports are not extreme to the kids who skateboard, surf, aggressively in-line skate, mountain-board, mountain-bike, snowboard, wakeboard, street-luge, snow-skate, etc. It's what the ordinaries and the media might call "extreme"—the doers call it skating, snowboarding, and so on. They just call it what it *is*.

Today, extreme is on every marketer's list, and overused in TV spots for brands of the wanna-be-cool. (Word of warning to advertisers—extreme is also a "barf" word among youth culture.) The so-called extreme style has started industries of its own, from footwear (Airwalk, Vans, Simple) to clothing (D.C. Droors, Alien Nation) to TV channels—you know, ESPN2—and the newly named XGames (even they learned that *extreme* was a no-no). Realize that although the alternative sports scene has exploded, it's not going away. Actually, the movement is global, as teens in Japan and Europe are dressing and playing like their American freestyle counterparts.

FOLLOW THE BOUNCING ICON

Sometimes trends that have lingered with youth culture can come and go with the mainstream, like the whole "alien" or "visitors" theme in our mass media. It's on our TVs, in our theaters, on our T-shirts, in our gift shops—and even feeds into our paranoia on the Internet. There was a rumor traveling the Internet that Nederland, Colorado, a small town still stuck in sixties signage and architecture, was inhabited by aliens. Why? We couldn't figure it out when we passed through. Yes, it had this Old West sleepy-town feeling, but aliens? Anyway, we are an inquisitive culture, and aliens and space invaders are just one more thing to obsess on. And why not? How can we resist that we are the only superior living species in this universe? In the mid-1990s, the media deluged us with shows and themes that challenged this thinking and sparked our imaginations. *The X-Files* and *Millennium* entered the TV arena dominated by *Star Trek*, and quickly gained their own cult followings. Films like *Independence Day* became the 1990s answer to the *Star Wars* trilogy. Or so it tried—the 1997 rerelease of the movie *Star Wars* broke all records, dethroning *ET* (our most-beloved extraterrestrial visitor) to become the highest-grossing movie ever.

Yes, the alien theme has been with us for some time now. From the rumored Roswell sighting to the 1960s *Lost in Space* TV series to the perennial worshiping of *Star Trek* by thousands of Trekkers, earthlings have been obsessed with visitors. But is it the obsession—and the entertainment world's manifestation of it—that is the trend, or the collective belief that what is real can be questioned? That there is no prepackaged "reality," that aliens can exist by the sheer belief that we want them to. The answer is the collective belief, the movement that has shifted through time and still exists today.

The TV shows, the movies, the trinkets and the green little creatures adorning baseball caps are just the visible traces of what is actually a need to "believe." Some of the trinkets and such could be viewed as a fad, a quick-passing preference for something that suddenly becomes popular. But aliens used as a cartoon, graphic and product name have not just been a quick-passing fad in the youth culture. Cartoons, video games and comic books have fed our global youth with the fantasy of aliens for a few decades. The alien as an icon has surfaced in alternative street cultures for everything from skateboards to clothing lines. Liquid Sky, an alt-culture lifestyle shop in New York City's Lower East Side, has an extraterrestrial as its logo. The store has created a private-label line of clothing, and the Liquid Sky silver visitor can be found in hip alternative stores around the world.

Alien logos like that of Liquid Sky in New York City
reflect youth culture's belief in visitors.
Photo source: "Mindtrends" video report.

The street's belief in aliens goes deeper than embracing cute icons. In our first Mindtrends report three and a half years ago, over two hundred young people interviewed from across the country said they "believed" in aliens—truly believed that aliens existed. Two years later, alien characters hit mainstream shops and *Independence Day* and *Star Wars* invaded our theaters. Yes, aliens are pop culture again. In our latest "Mindtrends" report, the alternative youth were still talking about our destiny and the belief that we were not alone in this world . . . even though aliens are now "cheesy" in mainstream, they have become part of our culture and everyday life.

It's obvious that what the street cultures are doing or thinking today will somehow wind up, in one form or another, in the mainstream tomorrow. The fun task is in identifying what that something will be, where we'll discover it . . . and what it will mean to our future.

You have the ability to re-create the real now—you get a different sense of reality—whereas now aliens seem to exist as real things—whereas before they were more sci-fi. And now you just accept the fact that there is no realness, so you can create any type of reality you want through this kind of engineering. This is what I consider, like, sorcery or magic from medieval times—and I see a return to that. Believing in these sort of things—the overall sense of reality has changed. I see people getting into things they wouldn't ten years ago, like psychic networks and all the shows about aliens. You want it all to be real and shit because it seems, like, better—it becomes part of the language and it becomes part of everyday life.

—THUY, TWENTY-FOUR, DESIGNER,
NEW YORK CITY

3

THE INTELLECTUAL CREWS

Before worrying about what's next, we need to relate and understand what drives street cultures. How do they learn or discover? How do we have a meaningful dialogue with these creative "heads"?

The word *heads* comes straight from the streets. It's a term used to mean "intelligent people who are into their own thing." Whether it be music, poetry, reform, art or business, it is referring to one who has earned respect based on their strength of independence. In case you're confused, its meaning has nothing to do with the late 1960s tag *head* that labeled Greatful Dead followers and hippielike, marijuana-smoking nomads. As a street term, *heads* is the definition of intelligence, and today's progressive youth have begun to use the words *intellectual heads*, *intellectual crews* and *intellectual gangs* to describe themselves and their peers.

This "intellectual" labeling may sound arrogant, yet it is not. Rather, it is a mind-set that promotes self-achievement, self-empowerment, courage, life education, change and results. Moreover, armed with this newfound attitude, it is apparent that these young adults realize their importance to the "big brands" and the corporate giants who control the economic purse. They understand that mammoth corporations now seek their (the

> I think, first and foremost, poetry circuits worldwide
> need respect—and this circuit here in New York City,
> with all the crews, all the intellectual gangs, perform-
> ing on- and offstage is about to blow your fucking wig
> back. I'm telling you that shit right now, because the
> street's going to come to your fucking yard.
>
> I really appreciate the love and kindness that I've
> gotten from the streets. Never, never do I forget the
> streets—because this is where everything goes
> down. I like to be on the ground floor instead of the
> high-rises, because I'm a firm believer that you
> have to leave one day, and you have to come down-
> stairs and ask where we're at [here on the streets].
>
> —BONZ MALONE, FORMER INTERIOR DECORATOR OF
> NYC SUBWAYS/WRITER AND CONTRIBUTOR TO
> *VIBE* MAGAZINE

street culture's) approval to continually deliver goods that will
translate to megasales in the mainstream. Their stance of being
intellectual says to each other, and to themselves, and most
importantly to marketers—who spend innumerable dollars for
in-your-face this-is-what-you-need advertisements—that they
can't be bought or fooled anymore by the hype. Being a head
means that you won't sell out and be told what to wear, what to
buy, what to eat or how to speak by anyone (or anything) other
than yourself.

But how can we say that today's generation is smart while
the rest of the media labels them slackers and gangsters? Why
is it that we, Sputnik, suddenly have the audacity to challenge
the age-old perception of youth culture—historically standing
for adolescence, immaturity and ignorance?

There are several reasons. But the most vital is that the
heads, a.k.a. the intellectual crews, are striving to dismantle

prejudice. We're not saying that there are no more biases, and that prejudice is no longer inherent in today's society, or that each street culture isn't a distinct, separate subculture. It's just that all of today's progressive youth cultures that we have spoken to—from New York to Los Angeles to Atlanta—are speaking about replacing the negative with the positive. Abandoning prejudices, whether race, creed or color.

In essence, today's street cultures are hoping to feed their "heads"—learn about cultures they've always been shut out from, experience rituals and traditions they never knew existed and tune in to philosophies they believe could help instill a global sense of community.

However, this mental transformation, surge of independence and sense of leadership isn't an obvious rebellion like the punks proclaimed in the seventies. They're all not screaming their ideology by wearing a blatant uniform like that of a black leather jacket, Dr. Martens and a multicolored mohawk, mainly because this movement isn't a pop culture phenomenon: *It's a mind-set*, the wire that connects all of the fringe cultures and adheres to each subculture's sense of independence.

Meet the "intellectual" street cultures that are shaping youth's future.

THE COLLECTIVE INTELLECT

This mental transformation within the street cultures, where you have a "meeting of the minds," is, above all others, the basic foundation for the Collective Intellect group.

Who are they? They are the group that are truly alternative; they are the musicians, artists, filmmakers and social activists. They're the new force of what we knew as hippies, love children, rockers.

They're the New Thinkers of our time. Ageless, classless—and, above all else, they believe in integrity. Making a mark in this world is more important than money to them. Beyond intellectual growth, which they seek in places like informative web sites and classic literature, they are on a mission to do their own thing.

> I want to rap, do movies, write, speak . . . do whatever it takes to get the point across. And the day I die, I want to feel like I really impacted the world. They'll have to write me down on some pages, the day I die.
>
> —GIPP, TWENTY-FOUR, ARTIST WITH THE GOODIE MOB, ATLANTA

The most aware, they pride themselves on being socially and politically correct; they are smart and conscious about being *smart*. You can recognize them, their antistyle is really all about comfort. They were the first to embrace the "old skool" look, wanting everything that was retro—three years before anyone in the mainstream, they recycled Converse One Stars and bought used jeans from Army-Navy surplus stores.

If they smoke, they choose "retro nostalgia" brands like Camel and Lucky Strike, not Marlboro. Not the type to frequent Starbucks anytime soon, they're apt to drink New Age caffeine in a small coffeehouse with a book or zine (underground magazine or newsletter) in hand.

Overall, they shy away from everything and everyone that is *trendy*. They don't shop at Barneys or go to Cancun for spring break. They walked away from MTV, and now (if they watch TV at all) they tune into mainly sitcom reruns (Nick at Nite), old black-and-white movies, and the Discovery Channel. They favor independent movies (such as *Welcome to the Dollhouse*), music and art exhibitions. And before they'll pay any entrance fee, they'll check out who's backing the event.

This mind-set is what you would call "green." They grew up on recycling as a daily routine, they are conscious of unnecessary waste and they actively support and respect the environment.

As a cultural force, the Collective Intellect lives predominately in urban epicenters. In short, this group has been influenced by several different products, movements and events. They have also begun several movements and shaped many events. Although we are not saying that everyone with a Collective Intellect mind-set is influenced by all these things, nor partake, use or believe in everything we have listed, our taped interviews for the last three years reveal that these outside stimuli have been commonly acknowledged.

THE SOLDIERS FOR CULTURE

> I'm more inclined to the people who are similar to those in the Civil Rights struggle . . . like the Black Panther movement, the Bobby Seals . . . those who didn't stand around and give good oration, but they were people who did things and made people see a difference and not just talk about a difference or a better way of life in the future.
>
> —JAMES, NINETEEN, COLLEGE RADIO DJ, ATLANTA

With all the independent movements, cultures, businesses, messages, etc., going on, there will emerge the collective minds that think, act and react for the sake of culture. These are the Soldiers for Culture. Driven by their passion, the Soldiers for Culture have an intellectual, spiritual and artistic soul mixed with strong, ethnic urban roots. The Soldiers for Culture are more globally and ethnically mixed; they are influenced by other ethnic forces and usually borrow and mix from all cultures to make their style. Their source is their "industry," whether it be music, poetry or film.

They are the new Beats, the hip-hop poets . . . the urban performance artists. The hip-hop poetry scene is booming in urban cities across America, and hip-hop poets are spreading their word in Europe as well. The most common hip-hop poetry venue is called an "open mike"—where any artist can perform, once they have "signed in" with the promoter. Most venues have an MC or host who runs the program, accompanied by a live jazz band that lays a rhythmic beat to the spoken word. (Tune in to the Nuyorican Poets Cafe in New York City the first Wednesday of every month.)

Poet performing at open mike night at the
Nuyorican Poets Cafe in New York City.
Photo source: "Mindtrends" video report.

These prophets of the inner city are young, ethnically diverse and wise.

Their message is one of alienation felt growing up in a world that promises them little in material or social terms. But they're not only complaining about it, they're doing something. Forming their own organizations based on artistic and social interests, they are finding that strength is in unity. As a group, they will succeed . . . a success based on respect, not money.

Like Bob Marley and Jimi Hendrix, they will affect the

masses who realize it's about the culture, not the music. They are tomorrow's entrepreneurs, forming their own businesses and coalitions, and readying for their future. As a mind-set, they share influences with the Collective Intellect and the Hip-Hop Nation.

I'm working on a production company that produces film, that publishes and represents music artists—that's the vision of the Black Star Express, a multimedia juggernaut. Because doing spiritual work works—some people do positive things like Snoop [Doggy Dogg] and Biggie [Smalls]. They do ups—they have flavor. We're like seek the funk, seek the soul, give us some spirit, give us some politics and not preach about it. It's just a way of life—know what I'm say? It's just life, if people accept what you do naturally, then this is it. This is spiritual. Just freestyle one second—take a commercial break with me. I don't talk to sisters who do the smoke [marijuana] . . . I go to sisters who sell the blunt and I don't really do that, and they feel the vibe and stop blunt smoking. Seriously—when you go through this other realm, you don't need that stuff anymore.

In our organization, you got the youngest is twenty-one, the oldest twenty-nine—and we want to organize it together. We want to go to South Africa to check the vibe, and we "organized" it and was fortunate to take five brothers and five sisters. It was an experience . . . in America, we have a separation of culture and politics. There, it's just culture—it just is.

The whole theory behind our organization is that there is this star called Cyrus B that can't be detected by sight, but somebody detected it—something they couldn't see. That's like Taoism—keeping to the darkness. Like, you're in a room and turn off the lights, and you found a book—you found the book—you, not the light. What we do is just this—we can talk about all freaking shit around next to finding more food and love for the world, because that's reality. That just is.

—T'KALLA, TWENTY-SIX, POET AND FILMMAKER, BROOKLYN

Movements and cues from the Collective Intellect and Soldiers for Culture that are influencing mainstream youth:

- "Vegans": demanding absolutely no animal materials—using totally synthetic or plant-fiber products

- Web sites for activists: collective activist gatherings such as http://www.webactive.com

- Rebirth of "Big Brother is watching you": the fight for encryption and privacy on the Internet

- "Gee-Wizardy" or Virtual Reality Modeling Language (the use of 3-D symbols as language)

- Vintage pop-culture icons like Kilroy

- Zen extremism: engaging in sport activities that bring a karmic, even nirvanic experience, such as rock climbing, off-trail snowboarding, mountain biking, scrambling, ice climbing, sky surfing, etc.

- Native American spirituality

- Rolled tobacco and ginseng cigarettes

- Independent and art-house films, including a cult favorite like *Naked Lunch*

- Malcolm X, Jerry Rubin, Timothy Leary (and the dramatic debate over cryogenically freezing him)

- Ayn Rand's *Atlas Shrugged* and the theory of objectivism

- Asian and Far Eastern cultures, like Tibetan philosophy ("A thread that goes through everything and affects everything . . . it's a natural way." —Tao)

- Rastafarian belief in linking past civilizations with the present life of peaceful tolerance, personal dignity and rediscovery of Ethiopian culture (embracing the colors of red, gold and green)

- Women leaders: Barbara Jordan, Maya Angelou; music artists like Erykah Badu

- Zines like *Minimum Wage,* a twentysomething lifestyle comic; free circulars, free postcards, free information

- Magazines like *Utne Reader, Wired, The Atlantic Monthly, Hemp Times, Vegetarian Times, Alternative Press, The Face*

- Creative writing: short stories, short films, poetry

- Art museums, art history
- Radio: NPR news, college radio stations with fewer commercials and more experimental music

What they're doing socially:

- Eclectic music venues: live instrumental bands that offer jazz and blues beat for poetry reading and performance art
- Teahouses: hole-in-the-wall places that serve herbal and root teas, natural foods, antioxidant drinks; also, little campus coffee spots
- Performance art venues such as Vodu 155 in New York City, which fuses art exhibitions, spoken word, live tribal drums and Haitian music
- Neighborhood bars or local clubs with live performances, not a "trendy" atmosphere
- Playing MUD, a chat-room Dungeons and Dragons
- Poetry and spoken-word readings: The arts are alive and well in this group, with the Beat revival emerging in every college town. The "real thing" venues are usually held in small clubs that have a jazz or blues reputation, not a Borders bookstore.
- DIY: working on their own business, their own little venue. This group is all about "doing it yourself," creating web sites, encryption clubs, poetry venues, short films, free radio and cable access shows.

THE HIP-HOP NATION

Hip-hop's more about your skills, talents, being creative . . . the whole art form. People have forgotten, it's been overshadowed by this rivalry of the East Coast versus the West Coast. People don't remember what hip-hop was really about—and that was about different cultures coming together and just expressing yourself, whether you're a dancer or graffiti artist, a DJ or an MC. That was the basis of hip-hop. Hip-hop is the only culture out there that you'll find people of different races.

—DJ SYMPHONY, TWENTY-ONE, LOS ANGELES

> Hip-hop is the lifestyle and rap is the music. Our lifestyle is one of the most soulful lifestyles . . . it encompasses so many things. It's not a black, a white thing . . . it's a culture thing.
>
> —MACK, TWENTY-THREE, FOUNDER OF *FORTY OUNCES AND A BLUNT* MAGAZINE, NEW YORK CITY

Hip-hop is the culture from which rap emerged, a lifestyle with its own language, style of dress, music and mind-set. Although born from the American black communities, the Hip-Hop Nation is a melting pot of African-American, Asian, Hispanic and urban (and suburban) whites whose main interest is the hip-hop music culture. Hip-hop is an art form that includes deejaying (or cutting, scratching and mixing of sounds and tracks), emceeing or rapping, break dancing and graffiti art, and originated in the South Bronx section of New York City sometime in the mid-seventies. Rapping was originally called emceeing, drawing its roots from the Jamaican art form known as toasting (putting rhymes to a beat). Deejaying is the manipulation of a record over a particular groove to create a unique sound. The DJs created sound specifically to be rhymed over, thus hip-hop was born.

The creative mixing of sounds in deejaying and the freestyle rhyming of words instead of lyrics is truly unique to the formulas of music we had in the past. Born on the East Coast, the hip-hop explosion spread like fire, making poets/rhymers and their DJs—no backup band need apply—millionaires.

The music became its own category, and rap was a red-hot industry, peaking in the mid-nineties. Everyone of color—and not—was enjoying a new music born from the black American culture—because it was *different*. Its pioneers and soldiers were young. They were rebellious, opening their own record labels and street-promoting their demos. They represented power, success and individual creativity.

They know their power now: Coming into their own, they desire luxury in everything. Everyone is courting them these days, from designers to automobile companies to liquor distributors. But to win them over, you have to let them *discover* you.

Tony, seventeen, L.A., sporting his personal style of
old-school afro and eighties suit.
Photo source: "Mindtrends" video report.

They represent a powerful purchasing group who propel the buzz of "what's new." Not only are they trendsetters, they are the masters of interpretation. The first to embrace a designer or major label, they make that label "big concept" fashion. Or, in their words, they "blow it up." This group instinctively knows how to borrow "influences" to conjure a "personal style." The style this group embraces reflects their interaction with the rough, gritty urban environment as well as their social status.

In the wake of Tupac Shakur and Biggie Smalls's (a.k.a. The Notorious B.I.G.) deaths, the Hip-Hop Nation was perceived as territorial, with the East Coast and West Coast "camps" supposedly holding fort. But the meccas of hip-hop are not just New York and L.A.; Atlanta, Detroit and Houston are some of the tightest emerging music scenes. What's important to these new artists? Staying close to their roots by "keeping it real." Armed with a message, they continually have a strong influence on mainstream suburban youth.

What interests them (remember—this will shift in time):

- Music: jazz influences into new mixes—trip-hop, jazz-infused hip-hop as fast as 220 beats per minute . . . "the ultimate dance music"

- Reggae mixing with hip-hop: "Chatty" and "Rub-a-Dub"

- Professional music artists: Method Man, Nas, Dr. Dre

- House tapes, demos, DJs and MCs (the head freestylers)

- Successful people in the "industry" (music business): entrepreneurs like Suge Knight of Death Row Records; Sean "Puffy" Combs of Bad Boy Records; Russell Simmons of Def Jam

- The industry "greats" from the early B-boy days: Grand Master Flash, Kurtis Blow, Melle Mel, Public Enemy

- Strong and successful women in the industry: Faith Evans, Mary J. Blige, Sistah Souljah, Queen Latifah

- "One Love"—unity and respect for one another; using words like "show me love" (respect)

- Luxury utility vehicles: Range Rover, Lexus truck, Jeep, Land Cruiser

- Major sports such as basketball and football

- Individual sports such as boxing and martial arts

- Their community: being true to their neighborhood ("'hood"); their friends, who become their extended family; local church

- Street promoters: groups who distribute "samples" or demos of new cuts, specifically to clubgoers

- Media influences: BET TV, *NY Undercover* ("because it's real"); *Martin* and *Moesha* sitcoms

- Informational publications for "411" info: *The Source, Vibe, Rap Sheet, XXL*

- The Last Poets: obscure seventies artists who are considered the grandfathers of rap, giving rappers "a point of reference"

- Soul with gospel roots, reminiscent of Sam Cooke—groups like Intro, Silk and Solo

- African heritage books

- The teachings and philosophies of Dr. Martin Luther King and Malcolm X

What they're doing socially:

- Freestyling: on street corners, in basements, in clubs; it's a return to freestyle "break dancing" and rhyming off the top of their heads

- Private parties: eighties-style clubbing with private rooms

- Underground music venues where MCs get together with artists and poets, like L.A.'s Project Blowed

- Clubs: large urban warehouse settings where the DJs are king, spinning the latest dance music

- "Chillin'" or hanging out with their friends, cruising around

- Block parties: community-planned party event, or with a group of friends

Famous Heads in History

Kool Herc
Grand Master Flash
Dr. Dre
Ice-T
Queen Latifah

THE SPEED GENERATION

> If at all possible, I would like to live my life to the fullest, with the biggest adrenaline rush possible. When you feel a surge of endorphins running through your blood, through your head—I don't think anything can top it. Life should be just one big adrenaline rush. I don't ever want to be in my fifties saying, Gee, I should have—I want to say, Yeah, I did that and I had a damn good time doing it. I want to say I did most everything—and did it with pursuit of adrenaline—natural, untainted adrenaline.
>
> —KENNY, TWENTY, STUDENT, NEW YORK

Playing far away from the everyday, they are the *doers*. You know them . . . labeled as the "skate rats," in-line "punks" and crazy kids who push new adrenaline rushes. They're the "extreme" target of many marketers who like to label them but can't quite catch them. They have their own code of ethics: the skateboarders dis the in-liners (skaters) . . . just because their feet are bound to their mode of transportation. They give props to snowboarders (hey, aren't they bound?), surfers and BMXers (it's all about freestyling), mountain bikers, rock climbers . . . different terrain, same rush.

Breaking all boundaries is their credo. They are the ones who take a radical, extremist (but don't call them "extreme") approach to anything traditional. Irreverent and antiestablishment, you can't get "in" with them unless you're one of them. No "posers" allowed.

They support one of their own. Most of the equipment they use or gear they wear is manufactured, distributed or endorsed by someone in the sport culture they revere. Big, bold brands need not apply (just ask Nike).

Everything sucks to them. And it's cool to suck. They have a cheesy, comical approach to American commercial culture. They are deeply affected by TV and the "disrespectful." Nick at Nite was created for them . . . and they're tuning in more to the Discovery Channel than ESPN2.

Their biggest ambition in life is to be happy—and if they're athletes, to be sponsored. It's their rebel freestyle drive that will force the bounds of traditional thinking as we know it. Get ready.

What influences them (as we know it today—may not apply tomorrow):

- Discovering new sports: Mountain boarding: skateboarding down a mountain ski trail or hill; trail mountain biking: performing freestyle BMX tricks on a mountain bike with super inflated tires; in-line basketball: basketball meets hockey, played with in-line skates on a traditional urban court; flatland freestyle biking: doing tricks on a BMX or freestyle bike, using only the urban terrain of street curbs, playgrounds, stairs, etc.; motor-powered snowboarding; wakeboarding: water skiing with a skateboard-shaped ski; strap surfing: surfing on a Windsurfer board with straps, no sail

- Independent videos on alternative "speed" sports like snowboarding, vert skateboarding, in-line ramp skating, wakeboarding, snowboarding, street luging, mountain biking, boulder biking, big-wall climbing

- Professionals within their sport are the local heroes: Sal Barbier of Elwood; Kareem Campbell of Menace skateboards and Coffee & Cream skatewear

- "Underground" or "basement" companies: those owned and operated by the riders, skaters, surfers, freestylers, the doers themselves; individuals who manufacture their own equipment, rides or gear

- Retro sporting goods like Vespas, BMX low-rider bikes from the early seventies with heavily ornamented handlebars; fat-board skateboards and long surfboards; skateboard-based scooters and box cars—all designed for speed

- The world of cartoons and old favorites: return of the Smurfs and Miss Piggy; fascination with cheesy fifties graphics and old brand icons like Elsie the Cow and Mr. Bubbles

- Comic alien graphics, decals, space-age comics that depict sexy, girly "alien" caricatures

- House and DJ-mixed music tracks: ska, jungle, hip-hop, break-dance beats, rockabilly punk

- Music: punk; hip-hop; retro rock from the seventies, like Kiss and Led Zeppelin; the return of heavy metal, like Metallica; girl punk-rock bands like Bikini Kill, Fluffy; alternative rock like Beck, Fishbone

- Their peers: retail sales people who are actually "in the know" and work within the niche specialty store

- Graffiti

- Industry and cultural magazines: *Transworld Skateboarding, Transworld Snowboarding, Big Brother, Thrasher, Crash, Slap, BMX Bike, Powder, Mountain Biking, Fresh and Tasty, Wig, Surfer, Snap, Tread, Orbit, Spin, Source, Rap Sheet*

- Comic books: *The Silver Surfer, Dark Angel, The Ghost Rider*

What they're doing socially:

- Engaging in their "sport" or freestyle versions of it: in-line skate basketball, "flatland freestyling" on bikes, skateboards and in-line skates in the local parking lots, etc.

- Attending local Pro-Am (professional/amateur) sports events that give them the opportunity to test their skills on verts, ramps . . . and the opportunity to get sponsored

- Hanging out with friends on the streets and in the local skate, surf, bike or outdoor specialty retail shops

- "Dance Parties": organized DJ-sponsored music venues, usually by invitations posted in skate shops, used record stores

- Frequenting local bars "that are dirty," playing pool or pinball and listening to a jukebox or live band

- Communal living: roommates and housemates who help support one another

Famous Freestylers in History

Stussy
Burton
Steve McQueen

THE CLUB KIDS

> "Who is that masked man? And where did he get all those toys?"
>
> —THE JOKER,
> IN THE MOVIE *BATMAN*

You could say that the Joker was the ultimate comic book club kid—playfully citing new limericks and tricking Batman with new toys. The club kids get their name from their roots— the underground club scene. Born in the eighties, the club kids are not the cocaine-sniffing Studio 54 glitterati who started the modern definition of "clubbing." The club kids are the ones who live playfully through their underground music "family" or culture they embrace.

The Rocket tattoo of San Diego band Rocket from the Crypt, who have a cult following.
Photo source: "Mindtrends" video report.

The club kid arrived with the advent of punk rock, the first and original DIY street venture. Punk rock was strictly underground, incubating within the small bars and venues that treated the first true rock alternative with respect. Punk's audience grew as the anger, frustration and antisocial anxieties of the youth culture re-belled against a bloated, post–Vietnam War society.

Club kids typically were the easiest to spot on the street, as they used their style as a means to shock, to disconnect from mainstream and to connect to their like. They also played with their style, always searching for the wild, the trashy, the tacky—for now. Less shocking is their current mask of nor-malcy, as they hide behind the Average Joe facade and mimic the regularity of the suburbs. Once everyone else catches on to their average look, you can be sure they'll be on to the next. Our guess—purity, simplicity, transparency, as they prepare for their trip into the new millennium.

The club kids are what you would call "skin artists." They tattoo and pierce, paint, and in some fringe cases, amputate and implant, using their bodies as instruments of communica-tion and provocation. The club kids are the most creative and fringe; today, they consider themselves "personalities." Every-thing is glamour, everything is fantasy.

And the more eclectic, the better. The street stylists helped clear plastics and shiny materials to invade the mainstream. With their love of the unusual, the club kids brought us into the techno craze and reintroduced synthetics to our life. Com-forted by childlike accessories, they desire to look like a car-toon or superhero. They made famous Hello Kitty and Kero Kero Kerropi, DJ Bags and Patricia Fields/NY.

Everyone borrows ideas from the outlandish, promiscuous club kids because of their audacity to be different. They started the drag queen craze among the young (and sometimes straight), invented raves for fun and climbed new heights with the designer drugs of the moment. To get inside their heads, you need to look beyond their style and understand what influ-ences a club kid—what turns them on.

What influences them (warning—influences may shift due to a changing viewpoint):

- Self-expression: Skin used as a canvas, as temporary body and face painting coexist with tattoos, scarring and body piercing.

- Unrealities: movies like *Synthetic Pleasures*

- Communal activities: organized parties and spiritual theme nights like the Moon Tribe party every full moon in San Diego, known to attract hundreds of ravers

- Mind-enhancing new age drugs like Ecstasy, Nootopic and magic mushrooms

- Gothic music, Gothic cult movies like *The Crow*; CD-ROM games and web sites like "Carmillo," a Dungeons and Dragons punk-Gothic game; and the role-playing game called "Vampire: The Masquerade"

- Seventies punk bands like the Sex Pistols; punk master Billy Idol

- Female music artists like Ani DiFranco (necklace and armband tattoos, has her own independent label called Righteous Babe)

- DJs from Europe who are spinning the latest "experimental" music: early eighties disco meets trip-hop, still at 220 beats a minute

- Hindi-hop: Hindu chants mixed with hip-hop beats . . . *Sacred Music of the Sikhs, Khaled, Musiques du Rajasthan* CDs

- Alternative magazines like *Cover, The Face, Detour, Surface, Paper*

What they're doing socially:

- Still clubbing: clubs or organized "theme" dance nights reign as their social release; On the rise again: Gothic nights, industrial nights and eighties disco-mania

- Ambient clubs: clubs with atmosphere like Sound Lab in New York City with low ambient music, vibrating couches and toys; Beauty Bar (also in NYC) that's like an old beauty salon

Famous Club Kids in History

Madonna
Boy George
Goldie
The Artist Formerly Known as Prince

WORD FROM THE STREET

Edgar Miranda, twenty-five, artist/activist/teacher and cofounder of El Puente
Academy, Brooklyn
  Interviewed by Walter Meade, Sputnik New York City correspondent, at El Puente
Academy, Alternative Performing Arts High School, Brooklyn

Edgar Miranda, artist/activist/teacher and
cofounder of El Puente Academy, Brooklyn, NY.
Photo source: "Mindtrends" video report.

Walter: What are you involved in? What's important to you right
now?

Edgar: I'm involved in life, living life to its fullest, living with my
people, living with full pride of my culture, living within my
community. I'm involved in art, activism and education, and
that's all holistically integrated to one another where one
complements the other.

Walter: Holistically?

Edgar: Holistically—talking your body, mind and spirit.

Walter: Tell me about El Puente.

Edgar: El Puente is fundamentally based on a lot of what I believe in. When I came for training it taught twelve principles of mastery of collective self-help, of development, of creativity, of safety, of peace and justice, of holism—and all of these principles that they talked about were about my life and it was a bug because I found a place that was about me. I found a place that was progressive, artistic and actively involved in cultural upliftment, community upliftment and was still human in the sense of keeping it authentic and keeping it real.

El Puente, literally meaning "the bridge," taught me how to bridge art and activism and I've learned to create art that speaks for people, and speaks with the people, not so much at them, but with them. This space here is mad diverse, we've done everything from holding conferences here to poetry readings to plays to dance performances to even elections and debates.

Walter: What is the best way for a company to get your attention?

Edgar: It's better for companies to invest in long-term projects as opposed to what I like to call "publicity shots." A publicity shot is great because you could put it in your portfolio or your press package, but it's more of a serious investment when you are part of the creation of an institution—of a cultural institution—of a long standing institution—of an organization that inspires and nurtures young people in communities through the arts—art that speaks to the people in a language that they understand.

Walter: What do you like to do socially?

EDGAR: I love to go to poetry shows. I like to go to underground mikes because that's where the raw talent is, that's where the real art is. You have artists that are creating and nurturing their talent because they believe in the passion of art, they're not going around saying, "I can't wait to own my Lexus." They're saying, "Can you listen to this poem I wrote—I still don't think it's there." They're writing three or four poems each night because they don't feel they're up to par. We have to create an alternative media that speaks to us, we have to start from scratch, that's why the underground scene is so rich, because it's unbiased—well, not necessarily unbiased—it's nonsponsored. It doesn't have an editorial twist to anything that's going on.

Walter: What are your media influences? Where do you get your information from?

Edgar: I don't watch TV because I don't have cable and I don't like listening to the radio because I don't want people to tell me what to listen to. Where I do get most of my information from is from word of mouth, underground magazines and most of the scenes I'm around. A lot of my friends are DJs, so I speak to them or listen to their mixes. I listen to music and get involved in cultural scenes that are not necessarily positive, but natural and progressive—something that's about development as opposed to destruction.

Walter: What's happening in the music scene right now?

Edgar: The music scene is in a serious retrospective move right now, many of us when we started to learn about technology were blown away by it and felt that we had to utilize technology in everything—drum machines, samplers—but it got to a point where it was overkill; now we're sampling sampled samples. I think the move right now will emulate the underground culture that exists—live music with lyrics that speak about what's going on right now, not necessarily what goes on in an inner city environment, but what's going on up here *(points to his brain)*. We're getting more philosophical, more theological, more political, more creative in what we speak about, because the ghetto doesn't only exist in a physical environment, it also exists in our mentality—it's a mind state—that's where the music is going. Instead of looking out to feel for things, it's going in—into our imaginations to speak about things that we never thought we would speak about.

Walter: What burning issues keep you up at night?

Edgar: A lot of the work I do is really oriented around peacemaking, and peacemaking is very dangerous work. Martin Luther King died and he was a peacemaker; Malcolm X died and he was a peacemaker; countless people died— peacemakers. It's the most violent type of work to find yourself in, but it is the most necessary work because nobody wants to take up that banner, nobody wants to take up that torch and carry it, and those who do are the righteous few and there are very few who are doing this work. That's what keeps me up at night—how do we deal with violence?

Walter: What's your feeling on corporate sponsorships?

Edgar: I worked with some of my young people and we did a show for the U.S. Open, they're part of a rap group. The U.S. Open wanted us to wear T-shirts, and the sneakers company name I'll withhold because I'm not about to endorse them now—but they wanted us to wear their T-shirts and I was like, Nah, you haven't put any money into our programs so I'm not gonna represent you just because it's a phat T-shirt that you're giving me for free. Quote-unquote for free! They have people who have multimillion-dollar contracts wearing a T-shirt, but they want my kids to wear them for free? I'm not going to be anybody's billboard, neither am I going to encourage young people to be anybody else's billboard. I'll support anybody that supports my community—I'm not talking about a publicity shot. If corporations don't take a moral, ethical stand they shall be the architects of this country's destruction—they hold the power.

Walter: So, what's next? Final thoughts on the future?

Edgar: The future? The future the way I would like it to be would be based on what *Star Trek* is like—the newest movie that came out, one of the most powerful lines that Patrick Stewart, who plays Captain Picard, said was when his costar asked him "How much did this ship cost? How much did you pay for technology like this?" and he replied something like this—"We, in the future, are not motivated by money anymore, we're motivated by the passion just to do it, because we like what we do, we love what we do." I would like the future to be like that, filled with people that enjoy what they're doing for the sake of doing it—not for the sake of a check, not for the sake of props, not for the sake of being on the front cover of a magazine, but for the sake of "Damn, that felt good."

Part II

The Mindtrends Shaping Tomorrow

Seen, heard and revered in the underground, the following Mindtrends are the collective thoughts and micromovements that will impress tomorrow's mainstream youth and influence the way they will dress, interact, consume and play.

4

ARTIFICIAL PLAYSURES . . . TOMORROW'S PLAYGROUND

In a swift second all reality is erased. It's not a process. It's a fast, short, constant experience. You watch a man in black turn into a purple dog. A yellow cloud of smoke emits white rain. A desert concave into a seventy-foot swimming pool and a building melt into the head of a serpent. Mesmerized by hard-hitting beats and sucked in by psychedelic digital images, you grab the remote control and realize you're watching music videos on M2.

M2 is the new station from MTV, and it's dedicated to the progressive "heads" and their underground music. It highlights obscure and emerging artists like techno artists Byzar and Omo. But most importantly, it's one medium that is showing evidence of a reawakened movement: surrealism.

Surrealism originated in Paris as an art and literary movement initiated by poet André Breton. Overall, it aimed to liberate the powers of the unconscious. Painters portrayed subconscious or dream images, and artists developed abstract forms symbolizing subconscious thought. Legendary figures such as Dalí, Buñuel and others were its driving force, and the 1928 surrealist movie *Un Chien Andalou* captured its message.

First brewing in Europe between World Wars I and II, the movement was a quasi-political reaction against the so-called rationalism in European culture and politics. Considered "anti-art," surrealism's emphasis was on creating positive vehicles of expression against what its proponents saw as the destruction of culture brought on by the so-called rational thinkers of the time. Surrealists rebelled against the norm—they sought to escape reality, expressing their fantasies through images juxtaposed with reality. Its founder, Breton, wrote about the place in the human mind where dream and fantasy would be joined with the everyday rational world we live in—"an absolute reality, a surreality."

> Everything leads me to believe that there exists a certain point in the human mind at which life and death, the real and the imaginary, the past and the future, the communicable and the incommunicable, the high and the low cease being perceived as contradictions.
>
> —ANDRÉ BRETON, *THE SECOND SURREALIST MANIFESTO,* 1924

The surrealist movement of the 1920s parallels what is surfacing on the streets today, as the new surrealists, the artificial playsurists, challenge the norm. They are creating radical—and often fantastic—new means of self-expression.

Shocked? Well, just look at RuPaul, the striking woman who is a singer, actress, model, endorser/spokesperson, TV and radio personality. He is possibly the best example of the modern day's acceptance of artificial playsures. RuPaul has assumed an alter ego by dressing like a woman—and the world doesn't even bat an eyelash. The world has come to view his synthetic reality as a reality, which is not only his reality, but has become ours. We, the masses, accept RuPaul as woman, and society and businesses such as M.A.C. beauty products and computer company NEC have promoted and proclaimed that RuPaul's reality is *normal.*

If you look at alternative youth culture through the decades, this has been going on for a long time. Tripping through the sixties with a "one love" outlook, society flirted with cross-experiencing things that were considered part of the opposite sex. It surfaced with Vietnam protesters and exploded at Woodstock in 1969 to the sounds and impressions of Janis Joplin, the Grateful Dead, Jimi Hendrix, and others. High on mushrooms, marijuana and acid, the free-love and peace movement became a world harmonized by homogeneity. Everything one sex wore, basically so did the other.

This sort of "crossing" in style continued through the seventies as polyester became the most important fiber of the decade and both sexes wore bell bottoms and designer blue jeans while doing the hustle to the groove of the Village People, the Bee Gees and Abba. No doubt that during this era you could distinguish between the sexes, as heavy makeup returned to women's faces and gold lamé halters became all the rage.

But when punk rose from New York City's underground and emerged from Carnaby Street and the King's Road in London, a radical mind-set and anarchistic fashion code emerged. Revolting against the establishment, nonconformity was blatant as neon mohawks, half-shaved heads, safety pins, ripped jeans, Converse high-tops, combat boots, dog-collar bracelets and necklaces became the urban military uniform. Ignited by groups such as the Sex Pistols, the Germs, the New York Dolls, Circle Jerks, the Clash and Blondie in clubs such as California's Masque and New York's CBGB—the movement (which would influence the skinhead subculture style and other antimainstream groups) would leave mainstream America hard pressed to distinguish between who was a woman and who was a man.

Another source of androgyny was David Bowie (a.k.a. Ziggy Stardust) and glam rock, which took fashion to new heights by declaring that flamboyance and rock and roll went hand in hand. Freddie Mercury of Queen introduced the homoerotic joys of flash femininity, and Kiss, like a siren out of hell, screamed the notion that hardcore heterosexuals could don seven-inch leather heels, wear shocking heavy makeup, engage in fantasy role playing and still be hard-rockin' megastars.

As radio-friendly heavy metal took the stage (a far cry from what the *New York Times* considered Led Zeppelin in the seventies, when a staff writer described their sound as "heavy metal falling from the sky") the world would see more long-haired "pretty boys" sporting skin-tight leather chaps, fringe wear and bandannas then they ever thought possible. This, however, was the mainstreaming of club culture, when pop-metal bands like Poison, Warrant and Bon Jovi were the idols.

The prevalent club movements from the sixties through the eighties were experimenting with gender. But it wasn't until the late eighties and notably in 1990, with the mainstream media's acknowledgment of the club scene, that gender-bending would once again be a cultural influence. For many, the success of eighties English hair and makeup bands, especially Culture Club (Boy George's band) was society's neon road sign into the freakish cross-dressing and drag queen underworld. This movement, which was completely seen as a novelty of sexual expression then, is far from shocking now. And let's not forget what Howard Stern looked like on the cover of his book *Miss America*. So you see, RuPaul is not an anomaly, but a part of the fantastical world alive in the club culture. It is there, the underground global nightlife scene, that the driving push for a new surrealist movement has begun.

THE CLUB SURREALIST

The club kids are the ultimate example of modern day surrealists. With their penchant for fun, they live out their fantasies in the clubs, the parties, and the shows, dressing like cartoon characters, space-age Raggedy Ann and Andy dolls, dominatrix queens,

Princess Leia—or whatever they wish. Underground parties have become the galleries—the open forum for fantasy. It is there that reality becomes surreality and comic book stories come to life as they act, dress and live through "make-believe" personas.

> I dress up because I guess I didn't like the dull humdrum of life . . . it was so boring to me. As a child, I was attracted to shiny things, like that lightbulb. I just wanted it, I don't know why, but I wanted it. I love fantasy. To me dressing up is a way of being a puppet—a living creature from Disneyland, a cartoon. That's what I want out of life—I just want to be immortal that way and inspire people. So shiny things, just let me have it.
>
> —T. Rex, twenty-three, club "personality,"
> New York City

The personalities of the club scene have inspired many purveyors of style, and the terms "club wear" or "club style" started as a major fashion movement in the early nineties. It was this nocturnal scene that fueled the techno craze of shiny, reflective fabrics, clear plastics for clothing, and childlike accessories, like Hello Kitty and teddy bear backpacks. Once techno and club drugs like Ecstasy, Special K and GBH hit the mainstream, the club personalities of course moved on.

But it's not all about playing dress-up or make-believe for the night—some of them seriously assume a new personality, like Richie Rich, a New York androgynous pop singer/personality. Known only as "Richie Rich" (we still don't know his real name) by friends and fellow clubbers, he believes that cartoons are the future.

Richie Rich, like many club surrealists, believes that cartoons are the epitome of fantasy. Why? Well, perhaps clubgoers in the late nineties are infatuated with cartoons and make-believe because they are looking for an escape from the dol-

"I'm a cartoon right now—
I'm not even here."

—RICHIE RICH, TWENTY-
FIVE, ANDROGYNOUS POP
SINGER/PERSONALITY,
NEW YORK CITY

According to Richi Rich, androgynous pop
singer/personality, New York City, the future looks bright.
Photo source: "Mindtrends" video report.

drums of reality. Or perhaps it is because this generation was weaned on Disney and TV-land. Or maybe it's just because they're bored. Bored with the oversimplified fashions of the nineties and disgusted by the conformity of the Gap Nation.

Whatever the reason, their drive to live in a fantastical world of artificial pleasures shows no signs of slowing down—only progressing as we surge toward the next millennium.

For instance, meet Michael Sears and Hushi Robot. They're not your typical designers, nor are they drag queens. Rather they consider themselves transhumanists, sharing an imaginative vision that blurs the lines between humanity and robotics. Together, they design over-the-top unisex clubgear inspired by Japanimation and gender manipulation. Calling their fashion "pop couture," they create everything from shellacked hairpieces to shoes, accessories and clothes. But beyond their "Glamour Overdose" collection, influenced by plastic surgery, Sears and Robot's pop-futuristic design concept is painstakingly indistinguishable from their desire to live in a world of artificial pleasures. So much so that Robot wears bright blue hand-painted contact lenses to give him a starry twinkle like that of an android, and Sears has drilled a diamond into his tooth that sparkles like a cartoon character's when he smiles.

Artificial playsures (accessories and more)
from Sears & Robot, New York City.
Photo source: "Mindtrends" video report.

Their desire to build a futuristic fantasy led Sears and Robot to open a shop in New York City on Valentine's Day in 1997. A sci-fi snapshot wonderland decorated with robots and gadgets, inside they sell everything from flight bags to interactive jump-suits complete with a television and electronic buzzy button. Overall, the store is for the high-fashion toy addict. But more importantly, it is for them, because their dream to build a per-manent synthetic playground has been achieved.

But where does the club surrealist's desire to live in a syn-thetic wonderland come from? Well, beyond the slew of movies, TV shows and man's proximity to the third millennium, it seems the buzz word today is Japan—the most technologi-cally advanced country in the world.

In 1996, independent filmmaker Iara Lee (sister of ready-to-wear designer Jussara Lee) released a movie that would pro-mote and reveal that technology is already being used to create a world of artificial reality in Japan. The film, directed by Lee and produced by George Gund, is appropriately titled *Syn-thetic Pleasures*.

Infamous in the fashion community and the underground circuit, the film presents a visual voyage from the real, to a synthetic reality, to computer-created experiences. Lee shows us natural forests, synthetically created indoor beaches and ski slopes all in the same environment and takes us on a trip where reality and fantasy are interwoven—sometimes to the point where it is undetectable.

But, overall, the movie taps into our human need to control nature and to overcome all limitations, showing us that technological innovations have now given us this access. *Synthetic Pleasures* shows that technology mixed with human nature will bring transformations in our environments (virtual reality, synthetic environments, etc.), in our bodies (genetic engineering, plastic surgery, etc.) and in our identities (smart drugs, mood-altering drugs, etc.) Reliant on the research of MIT scientists, futurists, transhumanists and now-deceased drug guru Timothy Leary, this film deals with the big issues—our relationship with technology, where this relationship is taking us, and how it will affect our future.

> I'm making a film about a group of kids who design their own society. They live in this abandoned building and they're ravers who pretty much have this very hedonistic philosophy, and so during the day they each have their own art; like, one spins, one's a filmmaker, one paints, one does this, one does that and they also sell drugs during the day and then at night they have this thing called the "pleasure dome" where they basically push a bunch of mattresses together and they do, like, Ecstasy and have orgies. It's not really sexual, it's more, like, sensual, they have a collective consciousness and so they're, like, a more evolved society.
>
> —UZZY, NINETEEN, CULTURE DESIGNER,
> NEW YORK CITY

Right now it is apparent that the denizens of the club playground, with their android outfits and Astro Boy playworld mentality, is the one culture that is leading society to view a new world. Yet, they aren't the only ones. Meet the urban surrealists.

THE URBAN SURREALIST

Unlike the club surrealist, the new world for urban surrealists isn't filled with cartoons and lollipops. They aren't eager to escape into an imaginary synthetic playland. The word *surreal* for these progressive heads has taken on a different form. Like the original surrealists, today's urban surrealists create their subconscious visions through art. And for some, the canvas has become their skin.

According to Adrian, a tattoo artist at New Skool Tattoo on the West Coast, the latest movement, and a movement which is extremely different from previous forms of body art—whether Western or Eastern influenced—is surreal tattoos. Influenced by graffiti, electronic tagging and computer-generated images such as icons and fractal spirals, surreal tattoos are considered the future of body adornment.

While these urban surrealists have chosen to illustrate their visions on the skin, surreal art has also been embraced by the intellectual street crews as a means to express their socioeconomic and political concerns.

For instance, meet Matt Reid, a graphic artist who has done illustrations in various hip-hop magazines such as *The Source*. Twenty-five years old, Reid lives in downtown Brooklyn and is a graduate of the School of Visual Arts in Manhattan. A year ago, Reid decided to start a T-shirt line as an accessible medium for his visions. Reid considers himself an urban surrealist.

"I use the word surreal because I show the unreal. But certain things that are unreal may be real in the future, or may be real now, but people don't want to deal with those realities," says Reid.

Reid's first line of T-shirts features apocalyptic illustrations. There are two designs in particular, 1999 and 2032. 1999 is an illustration that shows the inner city before a revolution. It is the image of ghetto kids gearing up for war. In this illustration people are wearing masks because pollution has gotten so bad due to the ozone and the lack of care for the environment. Also, you'll see social security numbers on their arms, because Reid says that he's heard that the two middle digits of your social security number can show if you are a minority.

1999 T-shirt graphic by Matt Reid, © Matt Reid, Everything Is Dooable.

The second T-shirt, 2032, is a visual of after the revolution. As Reid describes it, "You'll see the difference between humans and aliens. The humans are living in a big bubble dome and wearing bubbles over their heads, while the aliens are walking around, wearing hip-hop clothes. This is suggesting that the aliens have become assimilated to *our* culture, *our* way of life."

The emergence of surrealism in art with a political slant is understandable as we enter a new decade and a new millennium. Unlike the surrealists of the past, however, artificial playsurists today have a great new tool to use: the computer. And it is with this tool that there is an obvious move to create virtual worlds in cyberspace. For many, however, this is not just playing a game, nor is it an escape. It is a voyage into a self-created and self-empowered reality where things that aren't real become real—with a mere click of a button.

THE COMPUTER SURREALIST

Any child entering grade school now has a computer class or a computer at home. And to teach today's generation of children, schools are using computer games as learning tools. In years to come, as is already happening with today's computer-literate generation, computer games will make the traditional family board games like Chutes and Ladders and Trivial Pursuit obsolete.

But the computer games that have attracted today's computer playsurists aren't mere simulated puzzles or games that send you to jail and make you pay $100. They are mazelike adventures and role-playing games where there is a voyage into an unknown, mysterious realm. These computer games simulate alternative realities where the rules of "real" life have no bearing. This, as you well know, is extremely more advanced than Pac-Man. And the more advanced, the more intriguing. And undoubtedly, the most intriguing games for today's youth culture are the role-playing games.

In role-playing games it's not just two players fighting each other in Donkey Kong or a game of simulated baseball. And it's not considered "surreal" because you can die instantaneously and be brought back to life again. (C'mon, that concept is as old as Tom & Jerry.) It's surreal because similar to the controversial eighties board game Dungeons and Dragons: it is about assuming a grandiose, empowered identity that has magical forces and does not have to conform to any of society's "normal" rules. It is about venturing into a self-made never-never land or jumping into a child's fairy-tale book where there are demons and villains to be slain and you alone have the power. Nonetheless, it is completely and seductively surreal and once you're inside, it is nothing but a giant playground.

> I also see a religious bent in gaming. . . . A lot of apocolyptic games have come out like "Rapture of the Second Coming," which takes place during the apocalypse with the anti-Christ ruling over the earth. (Do you think it's because of the upcoming millenium?) Yes, it's an optimal time to be putting out a horror game with heavy religious bents. The Book of Revelation, in my opinion, is the premium horror story of all times, because it's got the ancient evil that's been brooding for the millenium, which is now rising up to conquer the earth. It's got everything you need in a horror story and a lot of people believe it.
>
> —SCOTT, EIGHTEEN, AUSTIN

Travel into the world known as Diablo, produced by Blizzard Entertainment. It's where characters develop by gaining experience and magical weapons as they fight through sixteen randomly generated levels of a dungeon bearing names such as Catacombs, Caves or Hell. All of the quests center around killing things in the dungeons, and with every death you, as the player, get stronger and smarter. You can cast spells; create fire walls and fireballs; call on an inferno or a holy bolt; create your own golem, which is a ghoul that follows you around at your command; have the power of telekinesis; randomly teleport yourself to another location within the game; and so on. And, in case you've mastered the game you've chosen, there are ways that you can join a guild. A guild in computer land refers to a group of players that have joined together and declared that when they play a multiplayer game they will abide by certain "elite and secretive rules." Ultimately, in a cult kind of way, they have chosen to form their own society in this make-believe computerized reality.

This role-playing game is one of many. The most talked about on the Internet are Quake, Doom, Mud and Obsidian. And if you're thinking these games are highly esoteric and only played by Gothic-looking or geeky kids who have nothing better to do, think again. Quake, a 3-D action game centered around a medieval/sci-fi theme, is so big that mega–rock star and cult figure Trent Reznor of Nine Inch Nails has furnished the musical sounds. Obsidian, in early 1997, realized its presence would furnish such an anticipated demand, it opted to run commercial ads during the most-talked-about mainstream TV show, *The X-Files*. And major youth-geared corporations such as Pizza Hut are so eager to get a piece of the financial pie that they are known to sponsor role-playing competition events for even small organizations such as the Local Area Network Gaming of Northern California.

Mixed with spiritual, scientific, space-age and good old-fashioned horror elements, these role-playing computer games have become the newest form of easy-access home entertainment for youth culture. In fact, in terms of visuals, surrealist Salvador Dalí would be proud. And, in case you're interested, these computer game manufacturers are so successful, they are multimillion-dollar corporations with major web site advertisers.

Today's computer-literate youth culture is also toying with gender on the web. There's a site called "The Make-Up Box" that offers the tools to change your identity, starting with a photo image.

With the Make-Up Box, you can change your appearance by "morphing" your features and voice to become someone else—and appear to be somewhere you're not by modifying the background image. Now you can assume the face and the gender you want over the Net. Hey—if you're not using real-time video conferencing, nobody knows what you look like anyway, right?

Trudy's not concerned. Trudy is a "virtual gender illusionist" who has a web site called "Trudy in Cyburbia" (which you can reach at www.datalounge.com/trudy/quiz/index.html). The site is devoted to Trudy's true-life adventures. (Note: We do not give Trudy a gender-related pronoun because, according to Trudy, the root of identity is your name, not your gender.) Within this web site is a corner called Draginatrix which examines the male "soul" and "assigns" it a thrilling new drag queen identity. Genetic females are also included—on the site they can become what Trudy calls a "Continental Casanova."

Trudy says: "So many private E-mails have asked how to start one's life anew and how to taste the world of another gender that I realized something had to be done—and fast."

But in case you're skeptical of the reality of a reawakened surrealism movement emerging from today's progressive youth culture, remember that today's youth culture is the digital generation, revealing themselves through techno music, graphics, animations and logos. Their aesthetics are visibly inspired by the computer, the germ of their visual stimulants. They have a natural acceptance of what is fragmented, fast and experimental. And unlike previous generations, they have an inherent new sense, a sixth sense—an addendum to their sense of sight.

So what is the key for capturing this playful unreality desired by tomorrow's youth culture? Understand the visions behind their surrealistic art forms. Beyond lights, color or humor used to enhance a product or message—have fun, create the whole experience, or at least the perception of one. Think of images, not words to tell the story. Pictures become language, as in the latest ads for Reebok produced by Heater, a Massachusetts creative shop. In a spot for the new DMX technology, the images were generated by a computer. Floating stingrays, throbbing and flowing petals of gel, liquid drops, colors and movements that evoke fluid—this was the experience on the screen. They didn't have to tell us that DMX was soft, cushioning protection—we felt the technology without having some big athlete describe it.

TOMORROW NOW

There have been few advertisers who have been able to tap into the surreal playsurist mind-set by projecting the unreal as the real. Yes, we're talking *Alice in Wonderland* here—the undisputed classic of the surrealist imagination. The distorted sense of reality of *Alice in Wonderland* is, in a sense, the perfect and profitable way to reach tomorrow's youth culture.

An example of this is Diesel Jeans. Their advertising (and introduction to American youth) in the nineties revolved around a celebration of the bizarre playfully poking fun at mainstream situations. Tagged "Reasons for Living," the Diesel ads reversed our codes of ethics with satirical pictorials, like the one of humans serving a roasted girl to pigs sitting at a dining table overladen with exotic foods; or the one with a bunch of pumped up "beefcake" males as human guinea pigs, floating in glass testing chambers, as fringe-looking people stand by like scientists "analyzing" them. It's not that Diesel tried to be weird. What they've done is tap into the street's stream of consciousness—that our society is too gluttonous (as in the feast) and our perceptions too phony (the beefcakes).

Also check out Nissan's 1996–1997 TV ads. They have come close by playfully twisting everyday realities. One of its ads shows a clone of that perennial toy favorite Ken taking a Barbie-esque doll for the ride of her life. Another spot shows a flock of wisecracking birds trying unsuccessfully to target a Nissan car with their droppings. Each time we are put into the driver's seat of an unreal situation, twisted to become a reality—we'd like to cheer for lucky "Ken" and mock the bad birds that bite the dust in the garage door.

And in terms of brands, the companies that will survive are those that adapt the fragmented view and deliver the "experience." Consider Lush, a London-based shop that sells bath and beauty products by the pound—literally. Personal products that our society packages so antiseptically like foundation, body and facial creams, eye shadows and lipsticks are scooped out deli-style from large containers and wrapped in nondescript paper packaging. Although the raw, industrial atmosphere is no-frills, some of the products have unexpected sensation to them. Like the bath tablets that fizz with effervescent bubbles (remember Alka-Seltzer?) and then explode with tea leaves and other organic herbs. Talk about a new twist to the soothing hot bath. With customers often lining up outside the door, Lush has earned a rep as the hip store in which to shop.

IT'S A SENSORY ALERT

So, what is the future going to look like and feel like? Well, this is the exciting part. We propose that in addition to a reawakened, computer-enhanced surreal art movement, the "juvenile" tendencies of youth culture will propel artificial playsures into everyday life.

Blame it on a need or urge, but living out a fantasy every day may be the only means to surviving in a world that is complex, fast and ever-changing. Today, street surrealists may thrive in the underground communities where people like themselves give shape to a reality that only exisits in their minds, but they are taking their toys and their games to the mainstream.

Everything we consume will have enhanced sensory stimuli—a touch, a taste, a smell or a sound. It'll be about the experience and not just the product. In fact, signs of it are already here. Check out the hip new clothing lines that offer sound bytes, like Moschino's sweater that "chirps" and Wild & Lethal Trash's T-shirt that, with a touch of the hand, repeats "I love you." Through sound technology that already exists in hand-held games like Game Boy you can infuse the fun sense of sound into anything. Imagine a soft drink bottle that whispers "Where've you been?" when you pop it open? Or running shoes that play your favorite tunes, or encourage you with the mileage, speed and calories burned?

So how will we communicate among these animated artificial products? Coming to a Hallmark near you: feel-good packages, small personalized multimedia products designed to be given as special presents. "Emotion Containers," a product of Phillips Electronics, deliver your emotions with a container that is personally scented, has a moving video image or message and other physical sensations. These packages will offer a sensory way of giving. *Why not say it with greeting cards?* WRONG GENERATION. We are looking at a generation that has new tools to express itself. "Just say it with video" is more like it. Stay tuned, as more products tap into this new means of digital communication.

Personal communication through multimedia applications? Just around the corner. Technology will connect us in bars, in restaurants and on college campuses. Electronic tags, personalized with your interests in music, media and free time will seek out others with similar interests. These electronic tags and devices that will adjust our moods and connect us to peers are feasible because the "thinking" behind them rings true to the digital generation. Hooked-up, plugged-in and byting back. Technology will eliminate all barriers. Perception or reality, it doesn't matter—it will soon be the same thing.

Beyond computers and synthetic creations, we will be inter-acting via our clothing. Tiny satellite-dish-like reflectors that are embedded within fabric will reflect light, our mood, sound and images. LCD panels will compute the outside temperature, the latest sports scores, our identification to the outside world. Sports apparel manufacturers already incorporate Illuminite, a fabric with a reflective thread, in everything from track suits to mittens. Scratch-and-sniff is next—in our clothes, shoes and accessories.

> (What do you think is next?) Television jackets. Could you imagine television jackets? Everything about what you wear, what your home's about, what everyone pushes down your throat all the time, what music you buy, who you are . . . if we can get video imagery into garments, you can project whatever image you want. We're going to eventually do that. Imagine if you can reflect out who you are to someone.
>
> —BARNEY, TWENTY-NINE, DESIGNER, PRO-TEK, LONDON

> I want to develop an interactive suit. A suit where you have your interactive communica-tions built in. You would have your telephone, a CD player, a computer laptop . . . all inte-grated into a suit. Atmospheric climate con-trols built in too.
>
> —CORY G., TWENTY-EIGHT, DESIGNER, CYBERTEK, NEW YORK CITY

If the technology is out there, we'll demand it—for the expe-rience and the convenience. TV-projecting clothing; lighted, glowing footwear; sound-emitting food. Life—and consumer goods—will become one big convenient vending machine, custom-made *anything*. Technology will allow all food to be preserved and eaten as a snack. Presto food. Also imagine that our moods, emotions and reflexes will soon be synthetically induced. With a whiff, we will digest a piece of happiness.

Right now, we create the experience with multiple drugs like Ecstasy and magic mushrooms; we stimulate mental clarity with the proliferation of Nootropics—smart drugs—and Nootropic-based smart drinks. But if we want to be like Mike (Jordan), fast as Superman and strong as Spawn, why can't we just sip, eat, swallow or slip on something that gets us there?

And since the key word in this freshly painted world we've presented is youth, just await the rush toward plastic beauty. Right now we have products that permanently tan, firm and eliminate. We can plug in the computer for assisted hair growth chambers and watch our locks grow. This need to morph—to transform—grows out of the desire "to look young." See the fantasy, be the fantasy.

> At a fetish ball in L.A.
>
> (What's important to you in terms of fashion?) I'm not into fashion . . . it depends on what my mood is—if I'm feeling provocative, then obviously I'm like this. (How is it that you come to be like this if you're not really into fashion? Is this not a fashion thing?) No, this isn't a fashion thing—this is Halloween. No, this is a spiritual thing—this is playtime, yeah. (How do you mean a spiritual thing?) This is my release.
>
> —ANGEL, TWENTY-TWO, STUDENT, LOS ANGELES

Virtual reality, artificial reality—call it what you want. Improvements in computer power and display technologies will only solidify our fantastical experiences. Scan your personal UPC code (with vital statistics, credit information and intelligence rating) and enter the game. The goal is to transform ourselves to enter another dimension. Digital cash, shopping, vacationing—it's here already. Soon we'll be able to smell and touch that garment or tropical resort. This enhanced environment will be so realistic you won't want to come back to earth.

Network and head-to-head gaming such as Warcraft II and Command and Conquer will pave the way for holodecks (personal virtual reality play stations) to replace computers. Tucked neatly in your bedroom corner, you'll step into a holodeck, strap on your immersion goggles and rack up those frequent playsure miles. Get onboard, we've heard simulated experiences are better than the real thing!

Whether they role-play or change personalities, the street playsurists are sampling our subconscious every day. Altering of reality and morphing to create strange hybrids is the playsurists' interpretation of the surrealists. Creating new languages, new music, new sensual experiences, the excess of sensation is the ultimate goal. Vivid and spontaneous experiences play out the unconscious expression. It's in this future world of playsurists that we will also relive our "nostalgic dreams." Think about it. The stage was set a decade ago—Tang, freeze-dried astronaut food, Pop-Tart breakfasts, microwave dinners, polyester. Consider what tomorrow will bring.

5

THE BIONIC BEING

Look, up in the sky—it's a bird, it's a plane, it's Super-man—redesigned! Not only on the big theater screen, but crash landing to a street near you is the sudden quest to become "super" (as in strength and perfection), the urge and need for *transformation*. Taking our bodies and our minds to another dimension—or at least attempting to through drugs, herbs, implants, exercise, clothing, equipment and plastic surgery.

The idea of the bionic being is unavoidable, as we become products of science and technology. DNA cloning, prosthetics, silicone injections, steroids—it's all out there and invading our personal lives. Face the truth—the bionic age is here. Instead of running to the gym, you'll be going to the lab for a dose of muscle and energy builders. Marketing rubberized wax chest plates that when heated harden to look like mean pecs? No problem. People with this mind-set are talking about technology and surgery that will transform them into that something they always wanted to be.

Having been pierced and branded and tattooed before mainstream youth, the street cultures will be the first in line for skin implants with time-release energy boosters or edible mixes of herbal and synthetic stimulants for hypermemory.

THE SUPER QUEST

Becoming super—as in transforming yourself to have ultimate strength and power—has been an adolescent fantasy since we can remember. In pop culture today, icons like Superman, Batman, even the Boy Wonder have bulked up to go head to head with comic book and computer game action heroes who are part human and, often, part machine—or what the tech heads would call "cyborg." The old Superman doesn't stand a chance against Ghost Rider, the Mighty Thor and the Silver Surfer—megacharged bionic protagonists who defend mankind with more lasers than Lex Luthor.

Interestingly, this bionic fixation isn't only for the male steroids. There's a gender twist to the superhero, as characters like Tank Girl and Dark Angel have reached cult status. Remember that sexy yet naughty Catwoman? The allure of the female-gendered superbeings are that they are sexy and strong—part of the "girls rule" mantra.

Take Marvel Comics' Dark Angel, for example. She's part human, part android, and wears a steel black suit that shows her bodybuilding shape. With her fire-orange mohawk-style hair, nose ring, female symbol medals and bionic powers that transmit powerful light energy, she zaps bad guys like the Psycho-Warriors ("men whose minds and personalities have been bleached out, re-imprinted and defiled by extraterrestrial parasites"). Dark Angel has other super female cohorts, often teaming up with the Wyrd Sisters ("daughters of the web-spinners who weave the fabric of the universe . . . the threads of which interconnect each and everyone to everything"). Wow, is this mother earth or what?

From cartoon fantasyland to the streets, aggressive girl athletes have been breaking into the guys' playground for some time now. The "strong yet sexy" street style started to take off in the mid-nineties as girls sought ways to express their aggression and power. Look at the surge in female snowboarders, skateboarders, aggressive in-line skaters and the buzz surrounding the WNBA. Beyond playing more sports, the notion of girls pumping up is gaining more and more mainstream acceptance.

Case in point is the 1997 Mountain Dew TV commercial with an alternative athlete doing totally outrageous tricks and in the end what you assume is a he is really a she. The guy's response? "Cool."

But for the street cultures, the trend of superhuman gender manipulation is developing into transhumanism (which basically is the transferring of sexual identity to become no one specific gender). You have to figure that this is the generation that not only still respects the Replacements (famous for their song "Androgynous") but grew up with pop culture *glorifying* androgyny with everything from Calvin Klein's "cK one" advertisements to genderless cult cartoon characters like Ren and Stimpy.

Young people have been scoping every means they can to transform themselves to act like part human, part machine. Their penchant for insane athletic "tricks" (like, ironically, the "Superman" aerial on a BMX bike); fat, bulky gear that protects and pads; high-performance athletic shoes; megadose carbo foods and pills for bodybuilding; and, most recently, their obsession with morphing their bodies, is proving that being "super" will be as second nature as "dressing down."

> I would like to be the Silver Surfer, a chromatic super-hero that goes around and beats everyone into submission until they do the right thing. (Girl friend interrupts) I know who I'd like to be . . . I want to be a bad-ass Japanime, double hundred Oko, so I can kick some butt.
>
> —STEVE, NINETEEN, AND BETH, EIGHTEEN,
> STUDENTS, SAN FRANCISCO

In *DNR*, a men's trade publication, designers submitted their ideas of what superhuman beings will be wearing beyond the year 2001. If Reebok and Nike have it their way, beyond the year 2001 we will be gearing up in athletic smart suits that give us speed, antigravity and protection. Athletic shoes will become "antigravitational molecular displacement sneakers" according to Reebok's creation, and our footwear will be combined into our apparel, with "porous acrylic contact activated toe pads" as designed by Nike.

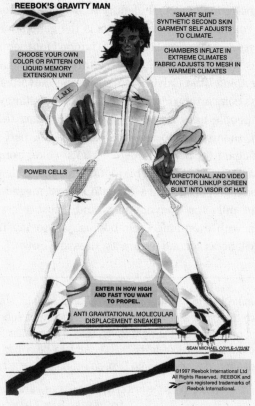

Reebok International's vision of the future. Illustrated by
Michael Coyle; © 1997 Reebok International.

Can we look forward to *The Six Million Dollar Man* becoming a reality? Although we have artificial joints, chochlear implants for hearing and retinal implants for sight, reality is that some leading scientists believe this will not come to pass within the next fifty years. Yet it's still the buzz on the streets. In our latest Mindtrends report, many of the young progressive heads have been talking about the issue of DNA cloning and body altering (especially since it was all over the media). Like stokers of the flame, they are wishing for the aging pill that will make them live extra years looking the same age. One twenty-six-year-old inventor has even created a freezer for a human head (see page 83).

Sound weird? The fact is that the streets are waiting for the next Frankenstein.

Yes, there are some groups who are nonbelievers in human cloning and bionic powers. In the street and lad cultures in London, there is a Gothic twist to the whole millennium change; some even talk of doom and destruction. Part of this is fed by the club culture, where the latest rage is a "Do not resuscitate" necklace. Will this reach American shores? It's here already in pockets of youth culture who are still awaiting Armageddon.

They are gearing up, more for survival's sake than for bionic powers.

The translation for the mainstream isn't that we will walk around as cloned bionic superbeings ready to kick butt. It's that we will be ready to accept and ingest things that transform and enhance our minds and our bodies.

THE BODY MORPHERS

For centuries, fashion has dictated that women must alter their bodies through artificial means in order to be perceived as feminine and beautiful. In ancient Chinese cultures women would bind their feet; during the 1800s they bound their waists in corsets; during the *American Bandstand* fifties women would stuff Kleenex in their bras; and during the sixties Motown era, women wore wigs and fake eyelashes. Even the everyday concept of wearing high-heeled shoes and makeup is a consequence of dealing with a forced cultural ideal.

Nonetheless, the desire to manipulate and alter the body is undoubtedly a mainstay—an ordinary, acceptable occurrence in today's society that still suggests wealth and prestige, and most important, is a sign of beautification. Whether it's merely waxing your eyebrows, investing in collagen-injected pouty lips or opting to surgically suction the fat out from your stomach, the truth is that you can create a "perfect" you.

Whether altering the body is right or wrong is of no concern here. The phenomenon is real, and today's youth culture is no exception. The reality is, due to the stimulants and occurrences in pop culture—the toys of technology, electronics, computers, virtual reality games, the shrinking globe, etc.—the street's move to morph and change is redefining our external acceptance of what is "beautiful."

You see, it goes beyond changing their exteriors; there's this need to forever blur the bounds of what is for guys, and what is strictly for girls. Beyond RuPaul, there is, of course, Dennis Rodman, dynamic athlete, multipierced, multitattooed and always toying with our opinion on his sexual preference.

From media, there's reality, and within today's street cultures there are obvious indications that relay their quest to go beyond the sex stereotype. Did you know that straight guy surfers and skaters paint their nails? In fact, there's even a men's nail polish now called Candy Man, made by Hard Candy. If you've ever been to a Marilyn Manson concert, you'd know that there are more guys carrying lipstick and wearing makeup than a gypsy bus filled with cheesy B actors auditioning for the remake of *Night of the Living Dead*. Surprised? Well, this isn't the half of it; the analysis regarding tattooing and piercing is so broad that we'd need another book to explain its entire link to the blatant ungendering of today's world.

In their playful way, the club cultures are using masks and surgical devices as accessories to completely hide their sexual identity and personality of their faces. In *Paper* magazine, Daft Punk, a young Parisian duo rocking the dance scene in Europe, were photographed wearing clear plastic face masks that make them look almost robotic (a look that seems to be in every photo of them).

Music artists Daft Punk are rarely photographed without a facial mask. Photograph by Dan Howell, courtesy of *Paper* magazine.

Remember when it was embarrassing to be caught wearing a retainer? Now retainers and other mouthpieces are considered "face accessories," altering your so-called natural beauty.

We know what you are thinking—there is no way the consumer or even tomorrow's youth will do this. But in one shape or form, they will. Because they *are*—with their facial and body piercing. Even in our coveted suburbs, hip kids actually want dental braces now that they come in a cool assortment of metallic or plastic (matte), bright or pastel colors. And what about nose jobs? Admit it—someone you know had theirs done in high school.

Surgical devices are becoming "face accessories."
Photograph by Dan Howell,
courtesy of *Paper* magazine.

Plastic surgery was also a heated topic in our last report. Yep, the street cultures are into that once Hollywood–Park Avenue tradition. Both men and women, club promoters and street stylists were talking about permanently morphing their looks. One stylist used Michael Jackson as an example. "If I want to be Japanese tomorrow, I'll just take care of that. Everybody will be doing it, I mean, why not?"

> You know how there's trends in tattooing and body piercing? Another direction that it might lead to is the actual manipulating of the flesh, and playing around with the flesh, making the flesh part of the sculpture. Making the body adorned by manipulating the flesh and designing right into the skin by force. Another series of pieces I'm working on are fishing line pieces. Fishing lines are strong (shows how he wraps a line around his face). It completely changes the character of the face . . . you're creating a personality by playing around with the skin. I think the next thing is plastic surgery . . . there are so many advances happening. The idea to completely recreate yourself is to reject—a rejection of God. Civilization through plastic surgery is going totally against what God created.
>
> —DESI, TWENTY-FOUR, JEWELRY DESIGNER/CLUB PROMOTER, NEW YORK CITY

Good question. The Body Morphers challenge our theory of acceptance and reject what is not acceptable in their eyes. What they will contend with in the future are traditional thinkers and makers of products meant for beauty and health reasons. Notice that they used the word "plastic" instead of cosmetic? If you think about it, what does the word *cosmetic* mean? "Cosmetic, *adj.*: designed to enhance beauty." In our interviews the word was "plastic," referring to the eighties heyday of phony, senseless surgery for personal gratification. To the streets, they are not looking to cosmetically alter, they are going for the "plastic"—in the colloquial sense, "unnatural, synthetic . . . so changeable as to be phony." Hence, the concept of "morphing," to create distinguishing characteristics, almost to become like a mutant or cyborg.

Get in line with where this youth mind-set is taking us. Beauty is beautiful to whom? And what exactly is beautiful? Want to sell cosmetics? Try calling your line "facial and body colorings and enhancers." Designing the next sunglasses? Think of head wraps for total protection—and character masking. Clothing with removable extra body padding? Comme des Garçons has been there, done that. The real underground designers are creating clothes that are like pieces of pliable armor that you can mold to your own sculpted look.

Edible skin colorants? They'll try it. Carbo-energized snack foods laced with steroids? We'll be there. What do you think Popeye ate—plain ol' spinach?

I think by the time that I turn fifty or sixty, they're going to expand our lifespan to 150 years or something like that. (How's that?) Oh, I have no idea how it's going to be done, but it will. They are going to find a cure to aging, and I'm going to be, like, fifty or sixty and I'm already going to be aged. And at that point there's going to be something like a pill or a cream that's developed, and I'm going to miss it, so I'm going to live an extra hundred years of my life looking old. People ten to fifteen years younger than me will look younger for the next one hundred years. So, then I'll have to get all this plastic surgery.

—DELIA, TWENTY-EIGHT, DESIGNER/STYLIST, NEW YORK CITY

With this youth's need to stand out, create character and go beyond their human frame, the sky belongs to more than Superman. As Andy in Austin said, "All I can say is look to the skies. Everything will be about satellites, it's all gonna be wireless—but it's also gonna be about space and us going to space. We'll start looking a lot like *Blade Runner*."

I think the work that I'm doing revolves around the history of technology in general . . . and a particular pursuit of longevity and the defeat of mortality. So, I've had an interest in various forms of suspended animation, various forms of preservation ranging from cryogenics to archaeology, and the work that I do usually displays those efforts mechanically. I consider myself somewhat of an inventor, and I build objects that function around preservation. Like this (shows small metal freezer). This is a prototype of a rudimentary time machine. It's basically a turbocharged fridge for cryogenic applications. This little fridge goes down to 135 below, which is pretty cool by freezing standards, and in that flask you would have a neural patient stored.

(What do you freeze in this?) It would be a human head (laughter). It sounds a little absurd. (But what is a head without a body?) That's the question—what is the value of a head without a body? Well . . . the assumption is that with fate and technology and future technology, there's bound to be means by which to repair damage and redeem that deanimated person, the head. Granted, there are technologies that could fix cell damage, there's technologies that can clone. Or in the future, a new body that can just as easily be downloaded into an electronic format so you may not need the body. That's where most of the hopes revolve for a neural patient—just as soon not be confined to a body anyway.

—JULIAN, TWENTY-SIX, INVENTOR/TOY MAKER, NEW YORK CITY

6

FREESTYLING . . . CATCH THE RIDE

This is the ultimate ride. The morphing of speed and sound, the rush of color and adrenaline with fluid, trancelike phrases in a repeated crescendo, subconsciously interrupted with the familiar swooshes and blips from the computer. This is the music, this is the style, this is the mind-set. This is freestyle.

Basically it is a no-rules approach. But this doesn't mean "freestyle" stands for chaos or anarchy. Rather, freestyle is a mind-set that is creative and spontaneous in nature. It is the mantra to do your own thing. Born from the music and West Coast sport cultures, freestyle has progressed as a total lifestyle. Unlike the words *extreme* and *alternative*, which were created by the media and marketers and not the "doers" (the actual consumers), freestyle is today's lingo, and a word that describes the moves, sports and music preferences. Freestyle is about everything this generation believes in: being an individual, doing something unique, being creative—living, working, acting, mixing *freely*. Freestyle is second nature to them—an innate sense of how they will live their life. To the rest of us, it's the next shift of what we call "extreme" sports, "alternative" music and lifestyle, "rapping" or rhyming, "individuality" in style—and the province of the new great "thinkers" of the day.

Freestyle means a lot of different things to different people. It is so inbred as a given part of today's daily life that it becomes something hard to define. Take the word "free"—ask anyone, and they have to think about it and then describe "free" as it either relates to them personally or in a global sense. Asking the streets to define "freestyle" is almost the same.

Freestyle is . . . I'm having a hard time explaining it. It crosses so much—skating, surfing, BMX biking, graffiti, music, rhyming, jazz—I mean, freestyle was the beginning of jazz. It's more than just those things—it's a lifestyle. It's the way you live, the way you work—it's just something in you.

—VICTOR, TWENTY-FIVE, DESIGNER,
NEW YORK CITY

Freestyle, for some of the guys, is that they're totally pushing it to the edge, to a point where you gotta wonder when that guy does some big, giant, crazy transfer from one ramp to the other, is it ingenious and beautiful skill, or is he just stupid? (laughs) Basically, live it to the fullest—right then and there—that's freestyle.

—CHRIS, TWENTY-EIGHT, BMX BIKER/AGGRESSIVE
SKATER, SAN FRANCISCO

I have yet to understand freestyle because I have yet to freestyle myself. It's only something that you can achieve individually—it's all up to you, accepting the limit. You're putting a limitation on yourself, then you're not freestyling.

—CHRISTINA, TWENTY-SIX, SKATEBOARDER,
SAN DIEGO

> Freestyle means do what you want, whatever you like—do it. Your own expression of your own style.
>
> —JOHNNY E., SEVENTEEN, IN-LINE SKATER, AUSTIN

Freestyle will be the street's riff for the new century. What the freestyler does is create a variation on an existing theme. As we move more into the digital age, with the exchanges of information and faster technology than we'll know what to do with, there will be the tools to orchestrate the improvisational impulse that will be an integral part of everything freestylers do. Visit a youth-oriented chat room on the Internet and you'll experience firsthand the ability to freestyle. They chat and dis each other faster than you can figure out what "FYFS" means ("Fuck you for sharing"). :-)

The ability to freestyle will become synonymous with survival, from the way youth will learn in school to the workforce to their everyday life. They are breaking the regimented, generational progress that taught former generations to be good citizens, follow the rules and obey the norm. The future will be about how individualistic, improvisational and creative you can be. The survivors will be the individuals who embrace spontaneity and are not afraid to marry technology with creativity. Moreover, the future leaders will come from the freestyle mentality . . . it will be their ability to mix their individual talent with the needs of the society that will create a new mode of behavior.

But how will order come out of their freethinking, free-form style? Let's first get inside their heads to understand the ways they are freestyling today.

FREESTYLE, THE SPORT

The birth of freestyle sports is credited to the fifties Southern California surf culture—the rebel "cats" of the day. Totally new, totally uninhibited, surfing became the newest craze among the teen set. In the sixties, another craze hit the California culture as surfers started "sidewalk surfing" or "board skating" the city streets, doing things like a "coffin" down hills (much like the sport of street luging, which is lying on a skateboard and "luging" down steep streets).

But as the boards progressed, so did the ride, from natural obstacles like curbs and concrete banks to empty swimming pools. Then riding changed forever with the invention of the "ollie," a trick that involves the combination of tapping the tail of the board down, jumping in the air while sliding the front foot up the board. You've seen the trick every time the media uses skateboarders—it looks like they are jumping or flying through the air with the board seemingly glued to their feet. Credited to Alan Ollie Gelfand, the ollie forever changed how skaters approach the urban terrain.

It's important to look at skateboarding as an example of a freestyle culture because since its first cruise, skateboarding has had an impact on every young generation—it has peaked in popularity, it seems, every ten years. From the first hit to the last rush in the late eighties/early nineties, skater "style" became a mainstream fashion statement. And suddenly every skater wanted to be sponsored, to turn pro. Skaters became superstars, traveling the world, raking in money from numerous sponsorships and landing on the covers of magazines. This influx of money into the "community" allowed young skaters to become entreprenuers. It enabled young kids to get inside the corporate structure and learn how it works so that they could be equipped with the know-how to launch their own companies. Because in this community, a real skater uses the real gear—authenticity is crucial. For example, brands such as DC Droors, Duffs, Etnies, Menace and Girl, and Chocolate are considered authentic, run by real skaters and made for real skaters.

The popularity of skateboarding also opened an industry in the athletic shoe market as little companies like Vans, Etnies and Airwalk boomed into Foot Locker, soon appearing on every "cool" kid across America. Suddenly, it wasn't enough to have the latest pair of Nikes—to carry the badge of "alternative," you had to have a pair of skate shoes—dubbed "athleisure" by the industry, "old school" by the kids. Yeah, the die-hard skate culture resented this boom, but it did open the door for the talented regionally known skaters to get some lucrative endorsement deals.

Ollieing and crashing through the generations, skateboarding has been a badge of rebellion—against authority, conformity and the traditional "win, win, win" attitude of team sports. This is the same mind-set that drives all the freestyle or aggressive individual sports on the scene today. It's also the reason that snowboarding, skateboarding, aggressive in-line skating and trail and freestyle BMX biking have exploded into mainstream youth culture. It's not a matter of how big or how fast you are, it's how brave or aggressive or individual you are.

> (How would you describe yourself?) Weird . . . I'm just a person who enjoys skateboarding, surfing, snowboarding . . . anything with straps. (So why did you start skating and the rest?) Because I wasn't big enough to play football.
>
> —RICK, TWENTY-THREE, SKATEBOARDER, SAN DIEGO

Their "play hard, have fun" credo will be the new way they approach so-called traditional sports such as golf and tennis. Think about it . . . how will they ever slow down for a gentleman's game of golf? And why should they? Look for these young "freestylers" to invade the courses and courts, pushing golf and tennis to new radical limits. If you are looking for the next action sport, look at how golf and tennis will morph and progress to keep up with the fast fury of youth culture.

In-line freestyle skater works the urban course of Central Park in New York City. *Video footage: Frederic Lilien.*

BMX freestyle biking is strong from the streets of Los Angeles to the Bronx. *Photo source: "Mindtrends" video report.*

Most kids grow up in a city, suburb or area where golf courses or tennis courts are out of their price range—or out of their sight. The recent surge in golf is because the boomers are embracing it—but what happens when the boomers move on?

Will the new freestylers move in? Maybe—but it will be on their terms, their way. Think the game will never change? Think there are no alternatives to the sport? Hey, it happened to the ski industry with snowboarding—which will become a recognized competitive sport in the 1998 Winter Olympic games in Japan.

> The whole point about Sub Par (an underground golf apparel line) is to just say, "Lighten up—golf sucks—just have fun." The whole thing is just about this (he points to the caddy image on his shirt). The PGA logo is a golfer, this is a caddy. This is the guy who humps and does all the real work and is probably a better golfer than the guy who's golfing. It's all about teens getting a pair of golf clubs and wanting to play the game, but they don't want to play it like their dads did and pay the big green fees. They just want to get out with a pair of garage sale clubs and just go hit a few and have some fun.
>
> —MATT, THIRTY-TWO, DESIGNER/GRAPHIC ARTIST, SAN FRANCISCO

The world of professional sports today has already experienced this freestyle attitude. Individuals from the most revered and successful franchises in the nineties "freestyle": Dennis Rodman, on and off the courts of Chicago; and Dieon Sanders, in the most macho of all sports, football. Even the die-hard sports marketing machine of Nike understands this new guard—in 1996, Nike sponsored "Radical Tennis" tournaments, a "no-rules" game played by some of the most respected professionals around.

As a marketer, jumping on this freestyle bandwagon with an in-your-face radical cool approach isn't your entry into the culture. You'd be shut out and laughed out. Remember, this is a tight circle, a community that crosses everyone who "rides" or "plays." An elitists' communal acceptance or brotherhood exists among their peers who play the same way. But it's hard to get *in*, unless you are one of them, or friends with one of them. You need to first start at the grass roots. Work on their level, supporting the sport in their neighborhoods. Accessibility is always an issue—especially since many communities have curfews or ban freestyle sports in certain areas. The key is to support and respect their sport, not glamorize it with ads depicting "awesome" moves and "extreme" overkill. Rollerblade, which became synonymous with in-line skates, knew its brand was too massive for the aggressive skate culture, so they created a sub-brand called RB. RB stays true to its roots, endorsing top athletes like Chris Edwards, quietly supporting the local competitions and exhibitions and advertising the product instead of hyping the lifestyle.

Again, if you're looking for the next action sport to hang your helmet on or to find something *new*, look at the *evolution* or the morphing of sports that exist. In-line skating is the evolution of traditional skates and ice hockey skates . . . wakeboarding is the evolution of surfing meets snowboarding . . . mountain and boulder biking is the evolution of off-road and road biking . . . and the list goes on. The nature of this speed culture is to creatively fuse something with something else—to make yourself go faster, jump higher. It's all about freestyle.

FREESTYLE, THE MUSIC

Freestyle, a DJ-based term that began with the rise of mixing in the late seventies, also ties its verbiage to the roots of hip-hop and rap poetry. In the underground club scene today, "freestyle" is the movement of melody and rhythm, the recombining of sounds that would normally not be mixed together. And it is not a preconceived or tested mix: It's mixing the sounds on the spot. For example, mixing a jazz beat with the super-hyper-electronic techno beat.

Freestyle, the prevailing new youth mind-set, has been underground for a while. The first true expression of freestyle was the emergence of jazz around 1900, the turn of the last century. Jazz musicians were renegades, creating a score with an improvisational—nonlinear—mix to make an ensemble work. Freestyle jazz was a variation on an existing sound; a free mix of rhythms and beats.

> What I'm seeing right now, you're getting lot of people moving through the hip-hop sound—trip-hop, which is kind of a jazz fusion mixed in with hip-hop—cool, neat sound, has a bit of that jungle sound to it—still has that 220 beat that's too hard not to dance to. Trip-hop is a relatively new offshoot—it's sound that you may be familiar with, but you also get a lot of the tenets of jazz and the freestyle movement . . . it's a movement of melody and rhythm, having ability to go anywhere . . . you've heard the sound before but it's been recombined with something a little fresher.
>
> —ROGER RAY, TWENTY-SIX, GALLERY OWNER AND DJ,
> LOS ANGELES

In the world of hip-hop, "freestyling" is spontaneous rhyming, or creating a rap off the top of your mind. Among young aspiring hip-hop artists today, freestyling is a favorite pastime when "chillin'" with their friends. Modern-day rap can trace its roots to the toasting or dub talk delivered orally over some combinations of reggae music. Kool Herc, a Jamaican DJ in the early seventies, is credited with the first freestyling when he recited improvised rhymes over the dub versions of his reggae records in the West Bronx.

Freestyling also crosses to the hip-hop poetics and the poetry crowd. It's creating a poem spontaneously, and is sometimes part of poetry slam contests. As we discussed earlier, from New

York to Chicago to Atlanta and L.A., the poetry scene is back. But these new Beats are all about "getting the info out," spreading the word about their culture, their world. Visit the Nuyorican Poets Cafe on New York's Lower East Side the first Wednesday of every month and you'll witness the new explosion as people from all walks of life, from hip-hop artists and jazz musicians to businessmen, catch the vibe of free-form expression. In fact, the circuit is exploding beyond the cities to the small college campuses, as poet collectives like Brooklyn's Vibe Khameleons travel the country and Europe to sold-out venues.

Beyond the hip-hop and poetry culture, freestyle is the future of the music industry, the mixing of rhythms, beats and electronic sounds, creating a new category temporarily called "electronica," "techtronic" or "techno." Rising from the underground, electronica: techno, ambient, illbient, trip-hop and jungle will forever change music. Techno started in the European club circuit in the early seventies and was imported as mainstream pop when the German electronic band Kraftwerk hit America. The club DJs started continent hopping as the demand for the underground electronic sound grew. Later, trancelike dance music gave birth to the rave culture.

In the early underground years of the late eighties, raves were held in old abandoned warehouses and other obscure places. There drugs, whether GBH, Ecstasy or marijuana, got the crowd high. But it was the frenzied, trancelike music that created a spiritual and communal dancefest.

Ravers in lifestyle could be seen as the new hippies. However, in style, ravers were and are the extension of the punks, the seventies subculture derived from the punk music scene so closely associated with anger and androgyny. The late eighties rave style—plastic fabrics, platform shoes, brightly colored hair for guys and girls—was considered fringe to the mainstream. This culture freed the youth culture from the anonymity of jeans and a T-shirt.

Today, electronica is going mainstream, as groups like the Chemical Brothers, Coldcut and Prodigy get hyped in mainstream media like *Newsweek* and MTV's *Amp*. We're also seeing the merging of the freestyle hip-hop mind-set with techno music, vivid colors and morphing laser imagery in recent TV commercials for Boss Jeans.

If you think that freestyling is prevalent only in youth culture's sports and music, look at what *Bring in Da Noise, Bring in Da Funk* did to Broadway in 1996. Its free form of tap, mixed with rap music, drama and spoken word, changed the face of the Broadway stage. Choreographed by Savion Glover, a brilliant twenty-one-year-old tap dancer, *Bring in Da Noise* broke all the traditional guidelines in the Tony Awards evaluations, because many couldn't decide if it was a musical or a drama—even when Mr. Glover walked away with the award for best choreography.

THE URBAN FREESTYLER

Freestyle is also the street term for what media tagged as "break dancing" or street dancing in the eighties. According to *Around the Way* magazine, the return of freestyle is like "a breath of fresh air from the gangsta and drug-dealers overload of recent years. Freestyle is free as in vibrant and fun, the partner of dance as an expression. Freestyle is style, the style of the people and a reflection of the flavor of their spirit."

Break dancing, which was originally labeled as B-boying, started in the seventies with the street gangs in New York and L.A., who used martial arts moves to defend themselves. The gangs or "crews" would have a stand-off of moves, upstaging each other in a sort-of battle of the dancers. Some of the earlier moves were called "Uprock," "Locking" and "Popping," which may be the closest to the first real hip-hop style of dance. The break dancing crews took on names, discovering that if they

Break dancer freestyling on the
streets of Los Angeles.
Photo source: "Mindtrends" video report.

set up a boom box and freestyled on a street corner, they could earn money. When New York City's B-boy originals the Rock Steady Crew hit the movies, break dancing went mainstream, fueling pop culture with Moonwalking, Popping, the Robot and other dances. The street crews became known as B-boys and fly girls, sporting their excessive gold jewelry, shiny track suits, gold fronts and Puma or Adidas kicks. Then the explosion of rap music took over breaking, and thus hip-hop culture became more verbally militant—without the dance moves.

But freestyling is back today as the streets are growing up, the culture is looking to infuse fun with a positive message and a new generation takes control—a new generation weaned on popular culture with its mass-produced hybrids, the mixing, borrowing and sampling of styles, tastes and success stories to create a "new" product.

For example, SmithKline Beecham introduced Lucozade, a sparkling, high-energy glucose drink, whose bright orange and yellow graphics are a playful twist on that other energy drink called Gatorade. Lucozade is another entry into the reviving New Age beverage category, as the industry recognized the need to capture this mixing, freestyle young consumer. Before we start thinking of how to transform our business to align ourselves with the freestyle youth, we need to understand how they will approach business, and eventually, impact our global marketplace.

KISS THE CUBICLE GOODBYE

Okay, so these freestylers want to do business (and many are already). Here's your wake-up call: Move out the desk, tear down the marketing pyramids and charts—and kiss the cubicle goodbye. Freestyle is more than the mind-set of this tight culture; it's a creative mantra, the code for doing things spontaneously, freely and without any preconceived notions or rules. In fact, some big corporations have realized that in order to conduct business today, they have to restructure their companies and adapt to the freestyle mentality. Words like "virtual office" and "virtual workplace" have entered our code of business, thanks to the portable notebook computer with built in fax and Internet connections. The ultimate freestyle setup, the virtual workplace is not easy for most businesses to adopt. The Chiat Day advertising agency was the first to go "virtual," with employees checking into the home base or office. But this idea of working whenever and whereever you like is not the only concept of freestyle.

What's going to change the workplace is the freestyle attitude, the free form of thoughts and ideas. Maybe you have had a structured opportunity to freestyle—in the guise of a brainstorming session. Brainstorming involves the tactics of free association, where individuals meet as a group to freely exchange and associate ideas. Some of the best ideas come out of brainstorming sessions, once everyone gets comfortable with the fact of breaking the norm—speaking random thoughts out loud in front of others. You won't have to ask the freestyler to free-associate, they'll do it naturally. Freestyle tactics will become a part of everyday business where the environment is open and creativity rules.

What the freestylers will infuse in the new guard of business is the rebirth of creativity—instead of target or strategic marketing, there will be creative marketing; instead of design or product development, there will be creative development. They are a digitally aesthetic culture, from their CD covers to their computer games to their street graffiti and tattoos. They grew up in a surrealist world, with color and sound and light that morphs into art. And they will bring this aesthetic to their businesses.

There won't be any cubicles or business titles or ethics about who does what . . . these freestylers will try to do it all. Everyone will be so busy freestyling ideas that this new business practice will create a need for consultants who can teach them organization and practical business skills.

Skeptical? Don't be. The freestyle office has been prevalent among young upstart magazines, independent young designers and web developers. Get it—young, because they are the future of modern business. And beyond changing the infrastructure and practices of business as we know it today, this freestyle mentality will also introduce a new quirky outlook that is evident by the marketing images these new upstart freestyling companies are presenting.

IT'S COOL TO SUCK

Today's freestyle generation is the generation that grew up with the one-liners, the media and American commercialism piped in through their MTV. They talk in sound bites and grew up in big brands like Nike and Reebok. They were bombarded with more infomercials, TV commercials and outdoor ads than any other generation of our time.

Often called the generation without heroes, their "heroes" are the underground, like cyberguru William Gibson or the antihero, the master freestyler himself, Howard Stern. Stern was the geek who said "Fuck you" to the system and now has become the single most influential person in media since Marshall McLuhan.

From his basement tapes in high school to his first college radio program, Stern has always been saying what's on his mind—no matter how "disgusting" or vulgar it may be. After college, he jumped from city to city, working in stations that were small and run down. But he developed a following, a secret cult that mounted to some ten thousand screaming fans outside his first movie premiere. He's the man. The freestyler who shut down New York's Fifth Avenue—not of his own accord—during his book signing of *Private Parts*. The man who (a) got his own nationally broadcast radio show, (b) interviews nude chicks and plays butt bongo with models and lesbians, and (c) is now listened to by more than eighteen million people nationally each day; the man who was a shy, awkward misfit his whole young life is now the leader, the king, the guru. Is this the revenge of the nerds or what? His spectacular New York opening of the movie *Private Parts* epitomized the glory of the underdog and the fall of plastic fork-tongued idols. As helicopters with blaring lights buzzed overhead and thousands of fans chanted Stern's name, the lead singer from the music group Marilyn Manson asked Stern on national TV, "Is this the Apocalypse or what?"

Yeah, it is. The weird, the alternative, the freestyle-my-style doers are this generation's heroes. They have ignited the greatest revenge—the underdogs take control.

So, how do leading-edge companies make their brand cool to a generation that believes Howard Stern is the ultimate? Make it the underdog. Make it lack confidence. Have it make fun of itself. No, it's not enough to be funny or to just use humor . . . it needs to be *uncool*.

In other words, do the reverse of what has lately been done

(What's cool?) Nothing anymore, everything sucks! (Why? Isn't it your job to make everything cool?) No, my job is to make everything suck. I do reverse marketing . . . kill your TV sets! No . . . it's just that everything's been done. (So, how do you market something with reverse marketing?) That's what the kids like—like "Sucks Skateboards." I'm going to open up a company called "Sucks Skateboards" and people are going to buy them.

—SCOTT, TWENTY-THREE, STREET PROMOTER,
SAN DIEGO

in advertising—avoid the in-your-face, try-to-be-cool approach. It just doesn't work. Case in point—a radio spot for the Mitsubishi Eclipse that asked the contemporary pop-listening audience to be "oh so cool" (yes, this was the actual voice-over), live life to the extreme in the Eclipse with extreme styling. Are we talking about a car or what?

Even in the club culture today, the individuals who shocked us with their colored hair, pierced body parts and sadistic dressing are now looking like the average Joe, sporting preppie sweaters, Jackie O. sunglasses and plaid trousers. That's the reverse of what you would expect them to be . . . it also makes them different, makes them stand apart from their shocking counterparts. It makes them cutting edge because they are breaking the rules, the stereotypes, the mold.

There have been small upstarts who broke the so-called rules and made a business out of it. In 1995, a small line of cosmetics called Urban Decay introduced the dark side of beauty, against the industry grain of pretty and pink. With street-gritty names for odd colors like Roach (a dirty name for a dark brown color), Urban Decay was worn by all the young and trendy mall rats. It even made the big house of Chanel launch the blood-red color

Vamp. Enter the dark side of beauty—which actually was a mainstream manifestation of the underground punk movement surfacing yet again. Sure, lines like M.A.C. and Bobbi Brown provided dark tones for all skin colors, but the hype that Urban Decay blasted was the anti of the beauty myth—the reverse of what we would consider "attractive."

Sometimes the use of reverse marketing is as subtle as a name—and only those who are in the know will know what it means. And sometimes those in the know will only know if it's for real. For example, Sal Barbier, a twenty-five-year-old professional skateboarder in San Diego, started a new line of clothing called Elwood. The logo has bull horns, reminiscent of a western cowboy theme. Yet the line was named for Elwood Johnson, an old blues man who never made it big. Elwood, according to the young team designing the line, should have earned his name on a Gibson guitar, but it went to Robert Johnson instead. They're giving "props" or respect to a man they thought was disregarded by our culture. Where is Elwood Johnson today? Who knows? He's not on the media hot list, not on the *Billboard* charts, and certainly not on everyone's mind, young or old. Why? Because he doesn't even exist. But this manufactured story made him the underdog, the low man out. And now the tight skate culture that follows Sal and company are emblazoning the Elwood name across their chests.

Often, the right move is to use a reverse approach in your message, big brand or not. Sprite soft drinks had the most successful use of a reverse marketing message in the 1995 campaign "Image is nothing, thirst is everything. Obey your thirst." The spot featured then-darling Grant Hill and a couple of regular kids on a court. They parodied the "Be Like Mike" syndrome (be like Michael Jordan) by blatantly stating that you won't play or be like Grant Hill if you drink Sprite—no matter how good or how bad you look out there on the courts, you still need to drink, so drink Sprite. Sure, the Sprite campaign has changed, but they have stayed true to the young urban street culture, saying that Sprite is nothing more than a soft drink, case closed.

To spread a reverse, just-one-of-the-guys message nationally, there are simple nuances that insinuate the message in a more authentic format. Companies without big marketing budgets are simply putting it in the packaging—the first blush of a brand's image, personality and integrity. The reverse marketing approach works well in a message that is intimately attached to the product. Take Kiehl's personal grooming products. Kiehl's is a company that has been around since 1851. Its simple, laid-back private-label-like packaging works—it says no-nonsense, just good plain stuff. They were the original before all the body and bath "naturals" came along. But to understand what they are about, you have to read the label.

Packaged in a navy blue plastic tube, Kiehl's "Close-Shavers" Squadron, the Ultimate Brushless Shave Cream, is *"a 'Hair-Raizer' Formula."* The name of the product is "White Eagle" and the copy reads: *"Fly Into a New World of Shaving Pleasure. Our most popular Ultimate Men's Shave Cream . . . Spiked with Menthol and Camphor, this superb cream formulation provides an incomparable skin effect for 'Close Shavers,' of a quality heretofore unknown."* The directions invite the shaver to enjoy the moment: *"Smooth on shave cream—no water needed—and glide your razor to the smoothest 'Take Off' imaginable . . . 'Try it, you'll fly it.'"* There aren't any fancy, organic terms to describe just plain old good stuff. Kiehl's taps into a witty sense of emotion, playing off the humor and fun factor for a boring daily regime.

In the candy aisles, too, you can find examples of products that are banking on reverse marketing. Instead of using sugar-sweet names, some companies are labeling their treats with disgusting names such as "Worms in Dirt," which are crunched up Oreos with candy chocolate worms in it. And the fun factor they equate is just what these kids ordered. But what can be next for this industry? Watch for an open admission, a know-thy-source approach as small start-ups deliver basically the same sweets but with a wry message—and openly admit they are just no good for you.

Devil Girl Choco-Bar, made by an upstart candy company, uses the reverse marketing tactic, boasting that the product sucks and that it's bad for you. Devil Girl is a cartoon-packaged chocolate bar covered with a bitchin' female character saying "Eat me!" The so-called "nutrition facts" section on the back reads "7 Evils in One!" and lists them in order:

1. Delicious taste
2. Quick, cheap buzz
3. Bad for your health
4. Leads to hard drugs
5. Waste of money
6. Made by sleazy businessmen
7. Exploits women

Sound too nasty for you? The candy industry isn't the only business impressing youth culture with this reverse marketing method. In a quirky new campaign, Miller beer introduces us to Dick, an underachieving advertising guy who apologizes constantly for not being creative enough, when you actually want to root for his honest, underdog style. Look for this marketing approach to appear on everything from cereals to ice cream to clothing and cars. Soon enough, reverse marketing won't be a tiny trend but a megatrend in advertising.

But how will freestyle and reverse marketing impact the future of traditional business? The big thinkers will think on their feet, not their seats—treading the streets, connecting to the mentality of youth. Open up meetings; use brainstorming as a standard; celebrate ideas. Test in the trenches, not in the focus groups. It won't be about how big the company is, but how innovative, authentic and different the brand appears. If the brand is number two or three or four—cheer it. If it's number one, play it down. This is what will get the brand *accepted*. Because a brand is an individual—it's all in the message, the packaging and the corporate culture that fuels it. Get mental, get real, think small, think entrepreneurial. Better start now, because the DIYs are coming to your front yard.

7

DIY: DO IT YOURSELF

The young street cultures today aren't in it for the money. It's the independence that drives them. Think about it . . . the job market is getting tighter, and the window of opportunities is closing. To get anywhere these days, you have to *do it yourself*.

The traditional mind-set of success was to climb the corporate ladder or go into business for yourself. The idea of battling the corporate ladder isn't even an issue with these DIYers.

> For the past five years I've been "entrepreneuralizing" myself—it's not a word, but I like the way it sounds. Entrepreneuralizing. Everybody start saying it.
>
> —WALTER, TWENTY-NINE, OWNER OF BLACK AS MANAGEMENT, BROOKLYN

Everyone is DIYing these days, from the Hip-Hop Nation of music promoters, writers and artists to the Speed Generation producing their own clothing lines and freestyle sport videos.

The fact is that the DIYers are coming toward big business through cyberspace at warp speed. Theirs is a tight youth culture with a mission—to be independent. DIY is their entrepreneurial creed. It's the mantra of the heads, the intellectual crews frustrated with the bureaucratic systems of today. DIY is their means of survival, keeping it real, spreading the word—and seizing the future.

To really get into their heads, spend a minute with a twenty-five-year-old who sums up the philosophy:

> I think what we're in the midst of now is a much more natural approach of looking at ourselves than actually happened in the sixties . . . this is the nineties, man, and into the next millennium. And the circuits that I'm running in are very similar to what happened in the sixties into the early seventies, but it's a lot more, because we saw history and we learned from history and we're taking it a step further. We're not just rocking fros anymore—we're rocking locks. We're not just rocking medallions anymore—we're rocking organizations. We're opening stores . . . we're much more on a natural tip. So the whole youth flip is culture, and gear that speaks to our experience and culture and gear that speaks to us and that's made by us . . . that's what the future is going to bring, because I know mad heads that have opened their own businesses. They got frustrated trying to emulate somebody else's style or trying to get into somebody else's organization—and they said, "Yo, I'm just going to start my own."
>
> —EDGAR, TWENTY-FIVE, ARTIST/ACTIVIST/
> TEACHER AT EL PUENTE ACADEMY, BROOKLYN

The medallions Edgar is talking about are the round medals that were worn by the protesters, the Black Panthers, the supporters of select civil and "spiritual" leaders in the sixties and seventies. To this youth culture, the so-called leaders gave them a purpose, gave them hope and gave them unity. But it was a unity based on a collective belief in the leader or leaders.

Where have all the leaders gone? Few new American heroes exist for youth culture today—outside of Spawn, Howard

Stern; William Gibson, who changed the lexicon of computers when he coined the term "cyberspace"; their music artists; and, for some, sports superstars. But look around the youth today . . . Dr. Farrakhan's Nation of Islam is going strong, but there are no more JFKs and no more Dr. Martin Luther Kings. Why? Mainly because this generation is skeptical: skeptical of government and of its leaders. In fact, they've been demystified by the concept of an all-perfect, no-ego, leader-for-the-people hero. They've watched too many superstars fall and too many broadcasts about the sexual perversions and corruptions of authority figures. And as a result, members of this generation, more than ever, look to themselves and their "crews," "communities" or "tribes" to institute change for the future.

Yes, we have always wanted to "belong" to a group or movement. We have searched for our leaders, rallied for their—or should we say *our*—causes. It's in our nature. But this culture is going to want to take control, to take their personal "causes" into action. Unlike the generations of the sixties, seventies and eighties who marched right into corporate jobs, this culture is marching and will continue to march its causes right into independent businesses. They are going to use the system—not revolt against it in an all-out protest—to implement a change.

DIY allows more and more people to enter into partnerships with one another. Alliances, coalitions, collectives . . . these are the businesses of tomorrow.

Check into New York City–based Bernadette Corporation, an eclectic coalition of an independent designer, fashion and film stylist, fashion-show producer and videographer who work independently but with the support of the "corporation." The vision of Brown University grad Bernadette Van-Huy, twenty-five, was to work independently within a network of similar interests, so that you can deliver the whole package or just pieces of it. No, they're not making money like other designers, but they've made

It's time for the younger people to take control. Like a lot of the old dogs that have been in the industry for a long time, they've been hustling, they made their money. But it's time for them to take off, basically that's how I feel. The reason why is because we're the new generation, we're the ones who should be out here hustling our market, not somebody else. We should be following our own generation, doing our own thing and setting the pace for everyone else. That's what I'm doing, and there are a lot out there that are doing it. Lines like Vinyl Grads, Junkies, Chick Wear, BC Ethics, Da Vinci, a lot of really good women's lines like Man Trap and Monodrama are doing it with their own flavor and still keeping it young. Young people on the team, young people designing, young people running it. They have it in their heart to push their own stuff and that just makes their companies even better—that's how we do it.

—LEAH, TWENTY-ONE, INDEPENDENT DESIGNER,
SAN DIEGO

DIY groups like the Bernadette Corporation in New York City share resources for selling and marketing.
Photo source: "Mindtrends" video report.

a name—referenced and respected by young designers working in big corporate structures like Liz Claiborne.

Everything in their future will be touched by the drive and

The generation today—everyone has three jobs, and they do, like, ten different sports, from snowboarding to skateboarding to surfing to mountain climbing to jumping off airplanes. (Shows his cargo pants) I can wear these to my office, wear these to a business meeting at my own company, I can wear them skateboarding and then at night I can wear them out at the club. So that's the way our generation is—everyone is involved in so many different things, and the lines between what's business and what's pleasure have been meshed. Think our generation—I'm 26—and the generation coming up is able to take advantage of this and it's really enjoyable. More of my people have home businesses.

—STAUCH, TWENTY-SIX, GRAFFITI GALLERY OWNER, LOS ANGELES

need to be independent. The streets are pushing us to become individualistic; the DIYers are paving the way. They will mesh the bounds of work and play—injecting energy, passion and fun back into business.

The DIY revolution is the manifestation of their freestyle mentality. DIYs will proliferate in the new creative movement; look at the independent DIY vehicles of self-expression: zines,

Stauch's creative passion lives in In Creative Unity,
a gallery he runs for street artists in Los Angeles.
Photo source: "Mindtrends" video report.

videos, independent films, underground parties, independently organized live music "showcases," graffiti art shows and so on.

The advent of the Internet and World Wide Web has appeased the youth culture's appetite for freedom and connection. DIY proliferates because whoever you are, wherever you are, the Web offers you a global forum.

NETTING THE STREET

The true success of DIY lies in the tight network that the underground has formed. Street promoters are a good example of modern-day DIYers. They are teams of local young individuals ranging in age from fifteen to twentysomething. Their job is to seed product, to get it into the hands of the local clubgoers, DJs, freestylers, street athletes, "trendsetters"—anyone mixing within the scene they see their product relating to. Street promotion grew out of the record industry, as executives employed local young clubgoers to get their newest releases played in the clubs—a new form of product sampling. These street promoters work on a project basis with companies like record labels; individual artists; soft drink, beer and alcoholic beverage companies; clothing and shoe manufacturers. The concept here is to get it onto the streets, to the grass roots. Although grassroots marketing or seeding product isn't new, it has definitely changed and grown to become a must-do marketing tactic. Because getting to the streets now also means getting and wedging your way into a community.

One of the tightest scenes that exists today is in Atlanta, with its exploding hip-hop and R&B artists, its rock scene around the colleges, and its growing club circuit. Keep It Street Promotions is an example of a start-up street promotion network run by Darren Davis and Talib Shabazz. They work closely with the DJs, club owners, industry labels like LaFace Records, and local artists who have made it: Outkast, the Goodie Mob and

Mista, to name a few. Work with Darren and Talib, and you're part of the family, the community. Through them, we got to interview the members of the Goodie Mob (some of the most inspiring intellectuals around); got serenaded by Mista at an exclusive LaFace industry party; interviewed Outkast; learned the "bank head bounce," a dance created by a local sixteen-year-old DJ named D Roc. We got "in" the Atlanta scene because we connected with Keep It Street, who help and promote local and visiting artists.

Grassroots marketing was the buzz in the late eighties, in the guise of product "sampling." But only a few businesses did it correctly. We know that it worked within the freestyle sport culture, as big brands began sponsoring alternative sport gatherings, such as Van's Warped Tour or Airwalk's Board Aid. But it's not enough to put your brand name on an event—this mind-set wants something free, and not from the big corporate bloat. The new word is street marketing—connecting to the street cultures through "one of them." Use the magic of peer-to-peer distribution—it worked in the freestyle sport cultures, mainly because the promoters were their friends. Street marketing helped hip-hop blow up. Artists were discovered in the clubs, introduced on the streets, played on local radio . . . and the rest is music history.

Companies that want success with tomorrow's youth are adding street promotion tactics to the corporate marketing mix. The goal is to get really close, starting now. With the expanding media opportunities of the future, with virtually hundreds of TV channels, thousands of BBS sites, chat rooms and web sites, thousands of magazines, zines and fanzines, street promoting will survive as the only true means of personally "spreading the word" to a niche market. The key to successfully marketing in the future is to be able to control the brand's impression on the street, to make it personable and accessible in this age of electronic communication and interaction. After all, a soft drink, a juice or a tea is a beverage—taste is the issue, not how wild the graphics are on the web site. The best way to sell a brand to this generation is to get the product into their hands, then they'll drive it, or wear it, or taste it—if they accept it.

Street promoting is the perfect example of how a major corporation can DIY—by not relying on the big advertising campaign to drive sales or launch a new product. Businesses need to get out to the streets, mix it up, DIY it. But be creative about it. Like Boss Jeans, who sponsored seminars for teens in urban community centers that introduced them to music producers and promoters. These seminars helped local teens learn first-hand how to DIY in an industry full of independent artists.

DIY isn't a new term. In fact, it was coined in the seventies and can be traced to the roots of punk. DIY was the means to buck the system, to control your destiny by being radically different. Then, punks sported a bad-boy, fuck-off attitude—they rejected the megaband concert circuit, played underground, and recorded their own records. They were the first aggressive DIYers. Punk stood for antivalue, anti–mass movement, and their torn, cut-up jeans, radical hair and black leather jackets with custom-painted images and buttons became their badge of badness. Jackets with crude lettering or surreal airbrushed images with names of their favorite bands became referred to as DIY leather jackets.

> DIY is funny. It can be applied in all these different ways. DIY is punk rock, you know? It's, like, we don't need these record companies. Let's get away from this sick corporate rock. We don't need to have stadium concerts. We can have this little bitty thing over here. Basically, DIY is "small is beautiful."
>
> —ANDY, TWENTY-SEVEN, FILM EDITOR, AUSTIN

SMALL IS BEAUTIFUL

Due to the fact that there isn't any one widespread movement like the punk movement, today's youth culture flocks toward tribes, subcultures that have niche tastes and niche lifestyles. Therefore, the future will be companies catering to niche markets within the youth culture. We've seen this approach to micromarketing just begin with the rise of specialized magazines. But now, with the growth and acknowledgment of thousands of zines, fanzines and E-zines, the strength of small, highly creative, highly connected and totally niche publications is skyrocketing.

The strongest example today in the publishing arena is *The Source* magazine. Back in 1987, a shy guy from Harvard University started a hip-hop zine, mailing out a few hundred copies. Today, that zine is *The Source* magazine, a "small" (by publishing standards) full-color monthly publication with a circulation of over 340,000. Still independently run by David Mays, *The Source* has made a tidal wave in an ocean of bigger, older publications like *Rolling Stone* and *Spin*. If you want to hold the hand of a streetwise, urban-minded sixteen-year-old guy, you can't get any closer than with *The Source*. Try to find it at your local Barnes and Noble, and guaranteed it's sold out before midmonth. Respected by the young street communities as the real voice of music, politics and social issues, their circulation is tightly controlled—keeping it real. Yet this small voice, through a column in the magazine called "Unsigned Hype," has been responsible for discovering new artists like the late Biggie Smalls (a.k.a. The Notorious B.I.G., real name Christopher Wallace).

When David decided to grow his little zine, he knew to hit the streets, using street promotion teams to distribute *The Source* at all the clubs and music venues. Today, every major youth-oriented company advertises with *The Source*—from Nike, Reebok, Adidas, Fila, Boss Jeans, Tommy Hilfiger and Polo/Ralph Lauren to Samsung and Sony, Mountain Dew and Sprite.

Started as a zine, *The Source* magazine discovered
artists like the late Notorious B.I.G.
Photo: Butch Belair, courtesy of The Source.

Probably one of the most successful DIYers today is Ani
DiFranco, a singer-songwriter and owner of Righteous Babe
Records, Inc. In an industry ingrained in politics, she bypassed
the standard ranks and self-produced her own label, grossing
more than a million dollars—enough to rattle the big guys.

There have been examples of the big guys trying to DIY. The
microbrew mania of the mid-nineties gave us a perception of
the DIY movement in the beer industry. Local breweries turned
into restaurants and bars, becoming the new "in" places to
socialize. The young and hip weren't ordering a Bud—they

were tasting local brands and sometimes even the establishment's own private microbrew. Taking its cue from the wine and new alternative beverage markets, the big brewers created their own microbrew-like brands to compete. And shops like America U-Brew provided the equipment and know-how for DIYers to brew their own beer. And as the microbrew explosion has gone mainstream, the underground has shifted to the traditional brands—what's new to them is beer in a can.

As New Age takes on new meaning, the trend toward niche beverages will fuel another microbeverage explosion in the form of locally grown teas and juices; fountain sodas will resurge as local "pop." We may be drinking mixed cocktails made with home-stilled vodkas, gins and rums that first hit the local parties. The new "in" places to socialize will be "houses," establishments that offer homemade food, local brewed beverages, hometown artists' music, local authors' books—and of course, the local linkup to a global surreal community—packaged and presented in an intimate, just-like-home setting.

Another example of a large industry repackaging into the "small is beautiful" mind-set is the tobacco industry. Whether we like it or not, there has been a steady rise in cigarette—and marijuana—smoking among the young streetwise sect, and consumer groups have proven it. You can argue the reason for this increase in tobacco consumption many ways—maybe even blame Joe Camel. But the fact remains that the tobacco industry knows its allure. They tapped into the concept and youthful acceptance of small, local brands, as Camel downplayed Joe and reintroduced Red Kamel (red being the color of solidarity, and the graphics of the package celebrating the working-class union); Moonlight Tobacco Company seemingly appeared out of nowhere (thanks, Marlboro). Small brands, but available at a convenience store near you. The true tobacco aficionados are smoking ginseng cigarettes or rolling American Spirit tobacco. Now that the class-action suit has banned the tobacco industry from advertising on outdoor billboards, watch them invade the Web, planting specialized campaigns or messages. One key to solid marketing strategy is to build a brand image as if it were small or localized, like the famous Snapple launch (before it was sold to Quaker Oats) that rang true as a small upstart. In fact, in their own businesses, these DIYers are bringing back the concept of bartering—exchanging goods and services. This appears to be the impetus for a widespread return to the small, niche, mom-and-pop mentality. We call it the "Jack and Jill" cooperative. Similar to the concept of a flea market, the Jack and Jill web sites or virtual stores will represent many independent businesses, renting space, sales and distribution manpower through a shared web site. And it is the introduction of using the Internet as a sales instrument that is propelling this notion. Cruise into independently owned web sites like Check-it.com (http://www.check-it.com), where you can purchase clothing, jewelry, music—all designed and produced by twentysomething artists. The site operates like a small-town store, as you select fabric, get fitted and look at unique accessories. No, its not just shopping over the Net—it's a personal shopper and designer catering to your unique style.

The DIYers with their freestyle notions will be changing the systems and the way we do business. They will push mainstream into thinking "small is beautiful" as we march away from the mall and hold a "click out" against the big corporate web sites.

DIY is a silent escape from the mainstream, from everything that is mass produced, mass advertised and homogenized. Like a bolt of electricity, DIY will zap the controlling strength of old corporations while fueling an explosion of underground capitalism. Old values of self-improvement and self-worth will proliferate among this independently created youth culture.

Independence is the future.

8

POSITIVE ANARCHY

The picture of anger, cynicism and angst that the media has widely attached to youth culture today is, as we pointed out earlier, almost nonexistent. What will replace this social picture in the near future? Creativity. A burst of creative expression that will drive the new youth culture renaissance—a positive anarchy.

Anarchy comes out of revolution and chaos, and it has always been a result of paranoia against government and the "establishment." But what we are talking about here, positive anarchy, is a logical revolution that is happening on the streets. It is anarchistic because it is a form of revolt, a break from the norm, yet it isn't driven by angst or cynicism. This movement thrives off of intellectual passion and it is a force bent on implementing positive change. Like anarchists of the past— those who ignited change by disturbing order—today's movement will liberate the great thinkers of our time.

Their underground revolution has been brewing for some time now, and you can see signs of it in the new crop of street graffiti. Symbols of unity (peace, circles, yin and yang) are mixed with positive messages like "seek the truth" and "one love." Many of the new streetwear lines are pushing a "mental" message instead of the huge logo on T-shirts and tops. Ecko

Unlimited sells T-shirts supporting a unity of intelligence: "seeking expression of the mentals for always."

T-shirt promoting "expression of the mentals"
by Ecko Unlimited, New Jersey.
Photo source: "Mindtrends" video report.

An example of this is today's underground poetry scene, which is proclaiming positive anarchy. Over the years, poetry has been the platform for revolutionary agendas from the beatniks to the Last Poets and Gil Scott-Heron. But now, instead of revolting only through militant lyrics, these young poets are spreading messages that promote positive action, teaching others how to evolve to formulate a positive mind-set. The Vibe Khameleons, a hip-hop poetry collective, is one poetry group that goes beyond traditional ideas of what expression is and can become. Not only do they utilize poetry, the poets become the poems, introducing "urbonics" to the scene ("urbonics," as coined by Walter Meade, manager of the Vibe Khameleons, means "urban phonics"). To quote muMs the Schemer, a Vibe Khameleon poet who has done commercials for Nike, performed in an HBO series and contributed his work to a book entitled *Soul of the Game* about basketball playground legends: "Revolution is not to be talked about. It's to be done."

Often their words are a call to open your eyes and your mind. One of muMs's works, "Kidnap the President's Wife Without a Plan," is about snatching the president's wife, taking her to a low-income housing development and forcing her to raise five kids on a monthly allowance of $240. She also loses her self-respect and dignity, and gets a cancerous growth on her neck "that saps her strength." In one stanza, muMs talks about taking her on the roof to "show her all the shit she doesn't own" which is, in fact, everything most people in that area do not own, like their homes and cars, "all the shit" the first lady—and a large majority of Americans—probably take for granted. muMs's poem is a perfect definition of positive anarchy. Kidnapping the president's wife may seem angry and rebellious, almost like "anarchy," but in the poem the process gives Mrs. President a reality check on another life, albeit one less privileged, thus delivering a "positive."

The poets write and speak from real life experiences, spreading their word beyond the hip-hop lyrics that talk about "gats" (guns) and life in the 'hood. The poets' 'hood is the poetry circuit, and they have toured the United States and Europe, including the Lollapalooza tour. Gun control, understanding Afrocentric beliefs, racism, poverty and spirituality are themes that lace their verbiage, as they often articulate a positive message through a highly creative venue.

Through their intellectual crews, organizations and leadership, the positive anarchists will funnel creative energy into issues, concerns, communications, in both the real world and on the Net.

Suddenly, we are taking control of our means to deliver a message, whether live at the Brooklyn Moon Cafe or by inviting a chosen few to participate via a chat. It's in these actions that we will see the so-called "protests" and "click-outs," (the boycott of certain web sites or chat rooms) rebelling against what doesn't personally interest us.

THE STRAIGHTS COMING TO A MALL NEAR YOU

The alarm buzzes loudly as Eric, twenty, rises to adjust his black nylon suspenders and tie his eight-eyelet black Dr. Martens. He cranks a song by hardcore punk band Minor Threat, wailing along with the lyrics.

Eric isn't getting ready to start his day—he's about to start his night. Decked in shades of black from head to toe, he wets his military-buzzed hair. Simple, almost crude-looking tattoos adorn his arms; words like "straight," etched in old English type, form an armband around his biceps. A simple black X marks his right hand. Eric is straight—straight-edge, that is. An avid punk rock fan who follows the straight edge of no drugs, no booze, no sex, no cigarettes, no meat . . . well, as much as he can.

Living in a small industrial town just outside of Minneapolis, surrounded by a youth culture of SHARPS ("skinheads against racial prejudice"), "townies" or college kids and gang bangers (mainly Crips and Bloods), Eric is trying to fit in and claim an identity. Eric is not the mainstream; he is the "straighter" version of the underground punk scene.

Straight-edge is a perfect example of positive anarchy. It grew out of the punk rock scene in the early eighties, when punk in the United States developed into a harder-edged sound called "hardcore," with bands like Bad Religion, Black Flag, Fear and Minor Threat. At hardcore concerts, which swiftly became accepted by the mainstream, there were drugs, excessive alcohol use, slam dancing and supposedly recreational sex. The straight-edgers revolted against this spiraling decadence, because their philosophy was, and is, that if "punk" stands for "antiestablishment," how can they continue? The masses had latched on to their irreverent ideology, the mainstream had caught up. The perception of punk would then have to be changed and become the complete opposite of what is considered "okay" or "normal." That being the case, it would have to reject society's decadence to once again emerge as "antimainstream." It would have to become "straight." The term "straight-edge" came from Ian MacKaye, then lead singer with Minor Threat. The new generation of hardcore punks would strive to become "straight": disciplined, conservative and spiritual.

> I don't drink alcohol. Try to be drug-free, and have been since I was a kid. I experimented with alcohol and things like that, but really don't like it. I feel that alcohol really is somewhat of a trend—they feel that they should be drinking, some reason to look cool. A lot of people need it to loosen up. Basically, alcohol, sex and trendy clothes just go together. Not my image.
>
> —SEAN, TWENTY-ONE, STUDENT, AUSTIN

> (Hey, what's that flyer all about?) Voodoo Glow Skulls, they're ska-core, which is kind of a paradox, since ska-core is ska, but I don't want to get into that really.
>
> (What kind of foods are you into?) Tofu, hummus—I'm vegetarian, like veggie burgers, salad, pasta, pizza.
>
> (What about liquid libation?) Don't drink alcohol—if you're going to drink liquid, you should drink something with some kind of vitamin in it. I like juice a lot, cranberry, orange juice. Anywhere I go, I'm going to drink juice or water, generally.
>
> —NICK, EIGHTEEN, STUDENT, NEW YORK CITY

The code for straight-edge is "sXe," the punk creed of absti-
nence from drugs, meat, alcohol and cigarettes. Straight-edgers
are usually "vegan" (totally against animal-based foods and by-
products such as leather) and are identified by a shaved mark-
ing on their head and/or a black X tattoo on the hand. The X
derives from the painted X mark placed on the hands of under-
age club- and concertgoers who weren't allowed to purchase
alcohol. That X became a symbol of going against alcohol and
other drugs among members of the straight-edge movement.

Considered a capsulated fringe movement, straight-edge lost
its steam in the mid-eighties when Minor Threat dissolved.
Later, in 1986, the movement revived with the New York band
Youth of Today, and other straight-edge groups like Gorilla Bis-
cuits and Shelter began expressing the ideology in their music.

Henry Rollins is the most commercialized image of straight-
edge today. A musician and spoken-word artist, he has a sort of
cult following, with web sites and fanzines, and a publishing
house named after his birth date, 2.13.61. A prolific writer (former *Details* contributor, author of several books and videos),
Rollins (known for his heavily tattooed body, especially the sun
that covers his back with the words SEARCH AND DESTROY) has
added acting to his talents, recently appearing in David Lynch's
Lost Highway.

Straight-edge has no denomination, and it is implied that reli-
gion and politics are your own choice. Ray Cappo of the band
Shelter is a punk-rockin' Hare Krishna, saying that Hare
Krishna was the natural step from the straight-edge movement.
Other bands that have taken this step are 108 and Prema.

As we discussed before, punk culture is considered one of
the true underground genres with roots in opposing the establishment and rebellion. Straight-edgers push a kind of positive
rebellion—similar to positive anarchy. This rebellion is against
fascism, racism and nationalism, believing that all people are
equal and shouldn't do harm to themselves (via substance

abuse) or to others. The rebellion is also against the obsession with material goods and money, part of the Hare Krishna philosophy. As two avid supporters of straight-edge write in their E-zine: "If the majority of people started acting up and following straight-edge rules, then the national power, which collects huge profits from 'legal drugs' like alcohol or cigarettes, would be weakened." (Word of caution to the tobacco industry: If antismoking advertising uncovered the right-wing lobbyists profiting from this addictive habit, who knows just how strong the industry would remain.)

Punk is the one anarchic scene that has recently returned and seems to bubble up to the mainstream every five or so years, as seen in the last couple of years with the success of Green Day and Rancid, both California punk bands who emulate the Clash, right down to fake British accents. And now in 1997, it's starting to surface again on the streets, as basic black, ripped and tight punk-style jeans, cropped buzz cuts and mohawks, black Dr. Martens boots, black leather jackets and the excessive use of metal link chains as accessories reappear. In some regions, like Minneapolis and the Hannepin Lake area, and Atlanta's Little Five Points, punk style has been steadily visible.

Unusual as it seems, these straight-edgers are slowly losing their tag as "freaks" and are quickly becoming seen as role models. Their puritan attitude comes as a relief to today's youth culture, which is constantly fed messages of self-gratification (drugs, sex and fast food) by society. It appears that their ability to follow such stringent, disciplined rules has made this subculture seem attractive, although somewhat extraordinary. In this case, this group is influencing a healthier bodycentric way of living—while socializing and existing within their select cultures of underground parties, raves and punk showcases.

THE NEW CONSERVATIVES

Although the philosophy of straight-edge grew out of the music, a derivative of the "straight" movement is spreading beyond the roots of punk culture. "Straight" is a street term meaning "cool," "good," "all right" and "for real." You hear it used loosely in the lyrics from all genres like hip-hop, R&B, heavy metal, punk, ska, and hip-hop poetry: music that is often misunderstood as dark and angry.

Besides the music's lyrical interpretations, "straight" is a way of approaching their next "phase" and their next "expression" beyond tattooing and piercing. There is a "cleaning up" happening on the streets. Expressions like "it's time to clean up our minds," "I'm cleaning up" and "straight up" are used to describe the move to change from their old habits of lifestyle and dress, and sort of "grow up" by cleaning up.

> The next expression is to clean up the old expressions. It's time to clean up our minds. We went through the Africa phase—we did it hardcore, we were flashy like a motherfucker. Then we got into the grunge, the filthy . . . man, you can't find a crease on the street, anywhere. Lucky if you could find yourself a bar of soap. But what's going to happen with the new rash of artists coming out now, because artists play a big role in what the youth do . . . everybody is into suits and slacks and things of that nature. So, everybody is cleaning up their act a bit.
>
> —JASIRI, TWENTY-SIX, POET, BROOKLYN

> The club scene here is getting really scary—they're into different ways to cut or better scar yourself. You can do a V, cut it on an angle, then cut it again at another angle. Apparently they get a rush out of it, they enjoy the pain. But I don't know how much that'll catch on. I think what's gonna catch on is being white-bread and normal—it's gonna be the most wild thing you can do. You're almost boring—just, normal.
>
> —DREW, TWENTY-SIX,
> TEACHER/GRADUATE STUDENT, AUSTIN

In our past few "Mindtrends" reports, there have been references, both visually and vocally, about "cleaning up," becoming introspective and looking more respectable. The most extreme case of this is in the club cultures, where the "suburban" and preppy look is replacing the trashy cyberglam and fetish wear.

Facial and body piercing is also moving under cover—literally. Now that every daring kid in the mainstream has a facial piercing, the underground are implanting their silver ornaments under their skin. The popular item is the barbell—usually visible in a piercing—surgically placed completely under the foreskin, on the forehead, the hands, arms, chest, wherever. You have to look close to see the visible bulge—and that's the way they like it.

NETIZENS KANE

Besides the walking, visible street cultures hiding their personal expressions, there exists another culture that is hiding (visually) yet planning to create a strong, virtual community founded on positive anarchy.

The computer—with the information highway to the Internet, the Web and anyone with an E-mail address—has clearly defined a new citizen of the world: "netizens." In the book *Wired Style*, netizens are defined as "members of the Net community, especially an active participant or member of a BBS, Usenet or IRC." Netizens practice "netiquette, the dos and don'ts of the cyberworld." The nomenclature *netizen* is an umbrella ID of the new world order, the positive anarchy that is seizing the Internet—and influencing our otherwise un-Netted world tomorrow.

People from street cultures who are into the power, ideologies and communities of the Internet are more like "Netizens Kane," a term borrowed from one of America's classic films, *Citizen Kane*. Impulsive and idealistic, the protagonist Charles Foster Kane becomes a publishing giant by proclaiming the power of information, and subsequently altering the way in which information will be perceived, expressed and controlled. But more important, his story showed how one person could seize that power for his own ends and by doing so could aid society (with a positive contribution) or hinder society (with a negative contribution.) Quite similar to the Netizens Kane, who will seize any or all information they can (by hacking) and spreading their powerful messages for all—or a selected few—to read.

As we all know, without an encrypted code, information, writings, stats and personal finances are available for all the world to see. It is obvious that the debate over "free information" and the impact it can have continues today in cyberspace.

In the coming decades this digital community, and the controversies that surround it, will define a new set of realities. This is a generation that will reward marketers who respect individuals' privacy and speak honestly and directly. This is a generation that will trash those who hide behind Madison Avenue's version of hyping things up. You can't pull a scam on cyberpunks—these Netizens Kane are creating the buzz. Like

Alan for instance, another Austin native who created the "Legal Pest of the Week Award" site. Every week, the site unveils names of companies that are pounding on small personal sites for so-called copyright infringement. Besides advertising the corporate culprits, the site also gives hints for the little guys to protect themselves.

Legal Pest of the Week web site for those who
harass free expression.
Photo source: "Mindtrends" video report.

The Netizens are the cybersoldiers—they have the powerful means to spread the message of positive anarchy. This new society of Netizens has had a slow start—the luddites, non-Netted believers in the mainstream—view the Internet as a foreign landscape, contradictory to their old-school beliefs in basic human communication. But the Internet is a vast network of human communication, and the process of setting up Netted communities has started and will continue. Beyond basic communication, what the Netizens are driving is the creative force achieved through technology.

Ideas are emerging from this Netizen world, ideas that are now only considered small and clannish in nature. But this is basically because most systems only have the means of allowing just so many people to interact on a site or line at one time—as opposed to the thousands and millions of people other media reach. But in the future, this tight, interpersonal network of communicating will not only be the wellspring for finding influential creative and business ideas, but will force or create a new definition of niche marketing. As we discussed earlier, grassroots and community-based programs will also become the new root of marketing on the Internet.

Don't fear the new rules. Just look back at the beginning of your roots. Every company at one time started small . . . entrepreneurial. The concept of newness, of filling a niche need, of coddling a core consumer, is what created the brand in the first place. As one of our correspondents put it: "You can't speak to the streets from the tower."

Nor can you effectively talk to the masses via the Web. Due to the vast array of sites, you can't expect one web site to be your access to the Netizens. In today's fragmented, digital society, it's all about personal preference. Give them real information, resources and the reason to link and connect further—without attaching a price or intruding on their privacy.

Just as we suggested hiring street promoters, companies will need a connected team of "Net promoters"—young individuals who chat and play and interact in custom rooms and sites, promoting your message. This is the goal behind Sputnet, Sputnik's newest vehicle to tap into youth culture. The real challenge is what that message is—since Netizens Kane (and perhaps, the rest of us) despise advertising intruding on the Netted world. Stay away from the *process* of advertising, and learn to integrate a positive message—whether you build "intellectual stations"; sponsor a cyberpoetry slam or fund the development of sites for microcultures—the success lies, at least at first, in *quietly* being there.

E.S.L.: ENCRYPTION AS A SECOND LANGUAGE

What the Netizens have propelled is a new language, born out of a computer culture who are into multitasking, doing more than one thing at a time. This culture is speaking shorthand, a fractured language, an English that smacks of codes and symbols. The next *American Heritage* dictionary that every marketer will need for reference—and for survival—is *Wired Style: Principles of English Usage in the Digital Age*. When communicating f2f (face-to-face, as in off-line), you can show your emotions without words. On the Net, your emotions are through shorthand like LOL (laughing out loud) or symbols like >:D (demonic laugh), >:P (sticking tongue out). More and more acronyms and symbols are being created each day, and the only way to understand what they mean is to be in the know.

Tech talk is in sync with the freestyling generation. It's fast and free-forming—and its content is abbreviated, meant for those in the know, or those who want to know, but not necessarily the nonbelievers. The word is "do-it-in-code," the street's version of encryption. Keep big brother, big companies, big non-thinkers—*out*. The streets have learned the value of using symbols, icons and encrypted "shorthand" as a means of spreading the word even before the use of computers. In its purest form, graffiti art is a "do-it-in-code" expression, translating the emotions of the street into images and symbols. Javier Michalski, a postmodern underground-rooted multitalented artist (painter, graffiti artist, graphic design) who has done work for Absolut Vodka and Nike, explains the reality and future of encryption, a modified language, in his essay "Abstract Oppressionism":

> Graffiti has spread everywhere; it is all over the planet, when people live on the moon, it will be there also. I vow that if possible the first "piece" [large scale graffiti pro-

duction] on the moon will be mine. The means by which these young writers purloined fame in an abject, poor environment has evolved into a brand that has indelibly impressed itself visually into pop culture: CDs, movie posters, TV commercials, half of all T-shirts, shoes, type catalogs . . . *ad infinitum.* Everything will be touched.

Graffiti is the single most insidious, infectious language I have yet encountered. Like all writing, it is everywhere. Though its greatest defining factor is that it is encrypted with the flavour: the flavour of "GRAF." This made all nonwriters illiterate . . . only those who spoke could see; only those who wrote could read.

Like Javier Michalski, who wants to be the first graffiti artist to paint a piece on the moon, the Netizens Kane will be the first to encrypt with pictures *their* messages on the Internet, thus "tagging" (as street graffiti is known) on-line. Graffiti has always been the message of street cultures, and the Internet is next.

Besides electronic tagging, they are making home pages that are more like 3-D objects than words or flat visuals. Coded VRML, virtual reality modeling language, is, according to *Wired Style,* "a protocol for creating navigable, hyperlinked 3-D spaces on the Web." Its code name on the streets is "gee-wizardry," their way of describing a rotating 3-D object that is meant to replace words.

So who is writing this new language? Self-proclaimed "cypherpunks" who write code to defend privacy. And since it's their privacy they are protecting, it's their code they'll write. Programmers and hackers, the cypherpunks create—and crack—the software or codes implemented by business and government. But their goal is not to crack and invade the world—it's to keep everyone out. As a cypherpunk posted: "Cypherpunks know that a widely dispersed system can't be shut down. Cypherpunks will make the networks safe for privacy. This allows for the possibility of a true digital persona—an "identity" permanently disembodied from one's physical being. Build it, they will come" (Eric Hughes, posted on "The List").

The European brand E.Play has recently toyed and designed with the cypherpunk tricks. A division of Fashion Box Group, which also owns the jeans label Replay, E.Play has a very shamanistic philosophy, gathering images and designs from all over the world, such as designs of ghagharas (traditional Indian skirts) and kurtis (short Indian tops), collecting the designs exclusively through E-mail. This system was supposedly invaded back in February of 1997 by a group of Afro-Icelandic hackers with unknown protocols who tampered with the blueprints of the E.Play collection, dispensing the data in the network. The E.Play team scrambled, requesting backup information from all its manufacturing facilities. The result was what they call "crypted" formulas for color, like akhadar green, and illegible images at low resolutions that imprinted on fabrics. The next month, some stolen images of a nuclear experiment executed by the U.S. government got registered in the E.Play operative memory by what they called a wild Europunk.

Already the trend toward encryption and encrypted symbols for logos are creeping into the mainstream, but we haven't yet seen the symbol or icon being the actual ID of a so-called brand—in other words, using no words. The first example of this in youth culture is the artist formerly known as Prince, who changed his name to: .

Some youth advertisers have recently used symbols to replace copy in their ads, such as the denizen of jeanswear Levi's, which uses icons of a "boy" and "girl" instead of saying "for men and women." It's also inevitable that the use of symbols or icons will be the replacement for company names, logos, brands and perhaps even personal names, as the rush to trademark has created a shortage of names to own in the marketplace. The challenge for companies will be to create symbols or icons or coded letters that represent and express a brand's personality, like RB, the aggressive in-line skate brand made by Rollerblade, XYZ skateboards and German couture clubwear brand W&LT (Wild & Lethal Trash).

Brands, especially fashion brands that have experienced logomania for the last two years, are beginning to place logos in "interesting," nontraditional places. Once the ubiquitous banner across the chest, brands such as Boss Jeans, Verso, Enyce, Karl Kani and Tommy Hilfiger have also begun to toy with logos and symbols instead of the actual spelling of their brand name. Of course, the goal should be to turn a logo into an icon status symbol like Nike did with the "swoosh" in the nineties.

To compete in the digital marketplace, plug into the street's sixth sense of graphics and colors and second language of symbols. It's not enough to create a symbol—look at CD covers, graffiti art and the ever-evolving crypted language of the computers. The symbols or icons for tomorrow's youth will not be those representative of the brand or a corporate ID tag—they will be those of the emotions and ideologies of the street cultures. To create a crypted message or symbol, look for images representative of strength, unity, peace, sharing, collective consciousness, intellectual celebration—the list can go on and on. But to be successful—and accepted in a fickle, youth-dominated culture—be true to their motivations. Be real, look creative, not businesslike.

The word is out—diic ("do it in code").

9

TECHNORGANIC

Austin, Texas, is perhaps the heartland of the technorganic movement—at least for the moment. It is one of the latest new silicon beds, driven by the young hackers and programmers. It's also a unique community set in a laid-back lifestyle. Travis, twenty-six, is one of the local programmers. What's his real goal? To live a minimalist lifestyle and to make a community that is eco-friendly but progressive in technology. He and some other local programmers are trying to set up a real movement—a cooperative community (E-mail: peace@travis.com) that would be able to sustain itself and have enough power—via linking up as a virtual community—to lobby the government or spread whatever the "movement's" message will be. Does he have a name for this community or movement? No name. Just a symbol to get it going. Travis says, "It would be peace and autonomy," as he makes a peace sign and crosses it with a closed fist. Travis and his friends are looking to take control, to go underground and underwire with force. Not by dropping out but by linking up.

What exists today—and will be growing stronger tomorrow—is a new generation utilizing technology to create traditions, customs and a sense of family and community. Unlike their counterparts in the sixties, who challenged everybody to

Travis Somerville of Austin shares the symbol of
his movement for Peace & Autonomy.
Photo source: "Mindtrends" video report.

drop out, the youth of the nineties will go down in history as
challenging everyone to link up. Counterculture is raving, Netting and moving together as a community.

The concept of community—organic and nostalgic—is thriv-
ing and being extended through technological advances. The
new communities that exist in cyberspace are strong, global
and growing larger every day. These new communities will propel creativity, political and social debate and entrepreneurial
endeavors. Today, when someone tells you to drop out, they
will usually tell you where and what to drop in to. (By the way,
it's called the BBS, the chat rooms, and while you're at it, pick
up your messages via your E-mail address.)

The real thrust of this movement is to understand that technology is not the driving force; it's the knowledge gained through
technology that empowers these new communities. Technology
gives access to those who want knowledge and a forum for those
who carry the message. The Internet helps us traverse time and
space; it fills our need, our spirited sense to expand—and connect into—a communal-like consciousness. Learning to tap into

We of the younger generation took the first step when we seized the technology from the exploding technological era which we were born into, and we empowered ourselves with it. But we didn't empower ourselves like those who came before us. We didn't buy into the dominator culture, the rat race, violence, or mass-media pop-culture cheese . . . we said "fuck all dat!" We took voice mails, computers, our Internet, turntables, amplifiers, the ancient art of trance dancing, and we made them our common ground; a creative sign of unity, rebellion, and responsibility. So now we're linked up, we all have the means of doing some major networking and supporting each other.

—RANDY, EDITOR; EXCERPT FROM THE WEB ZINE *FUTURE HARMONIX*, HTTP://WWW.PHOTON.NET/HARMONIX/ HARMONIX@PHOTON.NET

technology will pull culture together into Internet communities. Communities of freethinking people with a unified purpose to develop new forms of networking and support.

This is the technorganic movement, fueled by the freethinkers who know it's time to seize the power and change what is wrong. Hackers—cyberpunks—are the underground messengers of new thought. They operate quietly in the shadows, their messages pirated over the wire or posted on a BBS. They are the electronic philosophers with something to say. Technology is their vehicle. They are the voice.

You may be thinking of them as "Zippies" (Zen Inspired Pronia Pagans), a hybrid of old-school hippies, New Age travelers and ecstatic ravers. But the real technorganics are freethinking, at one with nature—and computer. The computer is an organic tool, a basic, natural means of communication. The technorganics embody the analytical sense of technology—the computer—with a spiritual, "one love" approach to business and their personal lives. By day, they will look like pacifists;

but by night, they are existentialists, hacking into the latest programs and creating their own virtual communities. Linking up with their likes—and dislikes.

> My academic work has really not centered around technology issues, but as much as the Internet is a community and is a network of ideas which emanate and circulate through media and through citizens, then I'm certainly interested in tapping into that . . . I think gradually also politics are going to be more and more influenced by the Internet and by new media. And of course politics now have been dramatically influenced by television, and there's lots of research out there that critiques and explains exactly how television has changed politics. The Internet and other new information systems are going to change politics once again and the interesting thing, the interesting possibility is that while television, of course, operates on the old "mass con" theory of people making the messages in some centralized location and they inject it into the public who sort of have to quiescently and privately consume them, with the Internet there is the possibility because of the interactivity of the technology for the public to generate their own political messages and to send them back up the pipeline and not only back up the pipeline but horizontally across to each other. So this is where we begin to hear the ideas of the virtual communities. It'll certainly be interesting to see how these virtual communities change politics . . . or start a new anarchy.
>
> —DAVID, TWENTY-FOUR, STUDENT, AUSTIN

No, this is not something small. Just look at the Wellnet, audio Internet show run by a company called Pseudo Sound. They have about forty-five hours of shows available, so you can go to their listing and choose a show you are interested in. All of the shows have to do with developing yourself—for example, they have an interview with a feng shui architect, and it teaches you to design the interior of your apartment to actually work toward better spirituality. Search for "feng shui" (a way of rearranging your space and life for more positive energy) on the Web, and there will be more than a hundred sites to choose from. But the power of Net-centric radio programs that are run by young entrepreneurs is that the interaction through the computer becomes more personal. As we spend more and more hours linked up in front of our machines, calming sounds, sensory stimulation and meditation "karma" screen savers programmed to give us periodic breaks will become a necessity in keeping us "fit."

TECHNOSHAMANISM

We've been talking so far about an organic link with the computer. Another organic link to technology is in the music—the interface between technology and spirituality. It's evident in the rave community, a place for techno nomads to engage in massive dance rituals and release inhibitions to amplified sounds of electronic beats.

This rave community links up to free the spirit—they put aside the material world and come together in dance to celebrate life in the moment. Like a Native American shamanistic ritual, performed by a priest or witch doctor to propitiate gods and spirits, foretell the future, heal, and so on, this community seeks out the liberation of mind incantations, trance dance, and sometimes drugs that heighten the senses and prolong dream states.

Based on rituals from our ancestral past, the rave takes us to a time when everything connected with human existence—our day-to-day activities—had a strong spiritual sense. But today, we mainly separate the day-to-day and the spiritual.

Technoshamanism is a futuristic concept that is about bringing the whole human spiritual self back into the everyday—our everyday technological advances. The philosophy of technoshamanism is perpetuated by the music group Qkumba Zoo from South Africa. Their music fuses tribal beats with electronics. The group's lead singer, Levannah, believes that today's youth culture is living in a transitional phase where we are still reliant on outside stimuli, similar to what Ray Cappo, Hare Krishna and lead singer of the straight-edge band Shelter, calls the "middle path." Yes, members of today's youth culture are moving toward techno music in search of an altered consciousness and communal sense, and they are embracing computers and newfound information. Yet as a result of our society's lust for disposable products, overconsumption and self-gratification, members of today's youth culture are reliant on alternative substances (Ecstasy, acid, mushrooms, pot, etc.) to reach those spiritual, enlightened heights. But true technoshamanism is being in a world where shamanistic rituals and practices are done organically and merged with the celebration of technology (music, information, science) in an effort to reach a higher level of consciousness. This technoshamanistic movement does not forget the sense of the individual. It's not a question of needing to go backward, ignore the powerful advances of technology and take up a Unabomber mentality, it's that we need to bring the whole human being (body/mind/spirit) into the technological age.

Another style of music with a mystical energy is trance. Trance, usually associated with Goa, is a ritualistic, digital occult that transports the dancer into what has been described to us as a ."liberating, rebirth state of ecstatic oneness." The current Goa trance craze can be credited to London (due to the fact college kids in England frequent Goa, India, during their "holidays" as Americans would go to Cancun on spring break).

The tropical beach settings of India, Thailand and Bali during sunrise parties or the jungles of Asia give this dance a more

> Our world is permeated with rhythm—the cycles of night and day, the seasons, the movements of the tides, the phases of the moon. All are examples of the rhythms that make our world what it is. As humans we have our own rhythmical patterns that are completely interconnected with these cycles: eating, sleeping, working, resting, etc. It is the rhythm of our bodies that keeps us going—the beating of our heart, the breathing of our lungs, the growth of cells. Everything is moving, everything is pulsing, everything is music. To be alive is to be rhythmical. Music is an extension of the rhythm of life, and dance is the embodiment of music—throughout the ages, music and dance have played a vital role in society, allowing for the celebration of life and the reaching of ecstatic states of oneness, both individually and as a community. When we dance together we are one together. As we raise our arms with an ecstatic cheer, we feel our connection to each other as one tribe united in spirit—the power of the collective. This euphoric dance floor release is as ancient as human existence stretching back through time to the original campfires.
>
> —"RETURN TO THE SOURCE"
> ALBUMS ON PYRAMID (UK)
>
> Promoters/Connections:
> Stuck on Earth 212.780.4614
> Solar Luv 212.629.2078
> Soundwave 718.670.3796
> Liquid Sky 212.226.0657

exotic, mystical and spiritual feel than anything that can be captured in a desert or club dance floor. No matter where the party, the sound of the trancelike music is electronically created and mixed, by DJs who have a technorganic frequency.

Trance music and dance emerged in the United States and

Britain as well as other countries about five years ago. Trance dancing is not a new social custom. Ancient tribes and native Indians have danced this way for centuries to celebrate, and today's disciples of Goa use Euro-techno-beats to the same effect to experience its new style of mystical, cosmic and spiritual "partying."

This exotic space-tribe music with its dance-drug-culture passions has spawned a street style, as young women—and some men—are painting their hands with henna, a primitive nonpermanent art form called mehndi from South Asia and the Middle East. Mehndi is the ancient practice of painting intricate designs on the palms or feet of the female.

Bindis, the Indian ritual of placing a jewel or dot on the forehead of a young girl who has reached her womanhood (started to menstruate), are the street beauty rage, and an extension of facial piercing (but it's less permanent). Mainstream youth today are wearing bindis mainly because it's been worn by some of the new crop of female music artists, like Gwen Stefani, lead singer of No Doubt.

Young woman wearing a bindi discusses Goa Trance with a Sputnik correspondent on the streets of New York City.
Photo source: "Mindtrends" video report.

Unlike the street stylists, the people who attend Goa trance parties think of themselves as idealists and purists, not fashion victims. They typically are seeking to live the back-to-the-source, cyberorganic lifestyle. The people who follow Goa trance and its spiritual, organic, earthy rush are technorganics, seeking to replicate an ancient dance ritual through the modern means of computers and synthesizers.

Once underground, the network of Goa trance has broadened due to the Web. Often the one and only link, the streets use the Web to get announcements on gatherings, reviews and new CD titles and reviews of the DJs and parties from all over the world: Sweden, New Zealand, Australia, the United Kingdom, Germany, Greece and the United States. One of the longest traveling Goa trance parties is "Return to the Source." The name

> Moving beyond the spirals of time
> We return to the source of love divine
> As we dance as one with the forces of creation
> The sleeping serpents will be awakened
> With these snakes of creation, our souls will entwine
> To dance this ritual buried deep within our collective mind
> Opening our hearts
> We surrender to the dance
> One tribe united
> We journey into trance.
> In this temple of love,
> We will dance
> As one.
> One body,
> One mind,
> One heart.
> Let the journey start . . .
>
> —"RETURN TO THE SOURCE"

implies the intrapersonal journey a trance can take you on.

There are some people who also argue that technology is becoming a substitute for these kinds of ancient rituals and trance dances. Virtual reality simulates the colorful, druglike escape; and the Internet is the ultimate way for more modern nomads to participate in a new tribal ritual of chatting.

And singing. According to Mark Pesce, the creator of Worldsong, there will be a three-dimensional place or web world where people can sing in real time in cyberspace. People will be able to enter the Worldsong Virtual Reality Modeling Language (a three-dimensional site), and gather samples of music from other countries. As you get more involved in a single country or sound, it will become finer and finer until you are communicating—or singing—with a single other human being.

MY BOLOGNA HAS A NEW NAME, IT'S V.E.G.A.N.

Move over Oscar Mayer—the vegans are coming. And you thought low-fat or no-fat was a threat. This youth culture has a large percentage of vegetarians, with a microgroup of vegans. For over three years, we have been tracking the references to a "totally vegan" lifestyle, in which you do not consume or wear or support any animal or animal by-products. A true vegan will not wear any leather, wool or fur, eat any dairy (because it comes from cows), eggs or any form of red meat, white meat or fish. In the majority of cases straight-edgers are vegetarians or vegans.

So it's beyond just what they eat. You could say that the athletic-shoe industry is lucky—most of their products are totally synthetic, although that may be more of a cost issue than wanting to be vegan.

Animal testing has been a major issue in the beauty and health-care industry, and we all know how successful Anita

I'd like to take this opportunity to perpetuate veganism because it has the lowest environmental impact you could possibly have. It's very good for the environment, if you go for animal rights and stuff like that it's basically a holocaust. Veganism, V-E-G-A-N, no dairy, no eggs, I'd just like to promote that I feel that's the best way to go, it's not gonna happen overnight but it's the way to go.

Right now one of my interests is environmental geology, I'd like to look more into that and see what fields are available. I'd really like to do something you believe firmly in that's great. I wish everybody would hold true to that. I've made a lot of sacrifices and that's what you gotta do if you want something to change. My parents go, "You're still a vegetarian?" They think it's, like, one day I'm gonna wake up and tell them, "Oh, yeah, I just had a burger at McDonalds."

—DAVE, TWENTY-ONE, STUDENT, AUSTIN

Roddick was at letting us know that the Body Shop's products were cruelty-free and socially conscious.

But many companies are realizing the benefits of using syn-

Lea explains why her Adidas are vegan.
Photo source:
"Mindtrends" video report.

I bought these Adidas shoes because they're totally vegan—I know Adidas didn't ' even think about it, maybe don't even care. But they have no leather on them—all synthetic. And they look good too.

—LEA, TWENTY-THREE, DESIGN ASSISTANT, NEW YORK CITY

thetics or natural fibers like hemp. Hemp-based products have been around since the sixties, but it's getting more limelight (hyped by activist actor Woody Harrelson) as a requested fiber. Hemp is used in everything from clothing to athletic shoes to backpacks.

The mass consumer trends of eating healthier, exercising and watching our fat intake have appeared to be mainly lifestyle choices of the boomers. Youth culture has been regarded as the fast-talking, fast-snacking, sugar-overloading boom, not boomers. But there's a change of course happening on the streets. They're sipping more herbal teas than soda, more water than juice blends. Overall, they are into this health aesthetic, and their influences go beyond their peers. Many of the emerging music artists, actors and writers—artists like Erykah Badu, Henry Rollins and Michael Stipe—are promoting their "vegetarian talent," as one guy called it.

> (What code you do live your life by?) Save the environment, it's not just about saving ourselves. We have to look beyond that—something that was here before you and me. Healthy living is also the way to be—like, I go on a guilt trip if I eat at fast food places. Personally, I don't know what love is, just 'cause I haven't experienced it yet. I kinda feel it through the artists I like. If all the songs and poems were written in vain, I'd be upset.
>
> —KIM, FOURTEEN, ATLANTA

Many of the youth we have interviewed talk about eating healthy again, part of gearing their body up while they feed their brains. Tap into the Internet, and you'll find hundreds of sites dedicated to the vegan philosophy. Most of them are club and college newsletters, poetry sites, recipes, on-line marketplaces for animal-free products and activist newsletters. (FYI, check out the House of Vegans site at http://www.voguelph.ca—if it still exists, it often mentions companies to boycott.)

The Vegetarian Youth Network is, according to its site, "an informal, grassroots, nonprofessional organization run entirely by, and for, teenagers who support compassionate, healthy, globally-aware, vegetarian/vegan living." Besides its site, the network has been mentioned in a variety of publications like *Scholastic News*, which is distributed to thousands of schools across the country.

Okay, so we'll admit it: The trend toward being vegetarian, or even vegan for that matter, is not new. But it is one that is prevalent among the progressive street cultures and the next wave of music artists, who, we know, are the major influencers. But the big picture here for tomorrow's mainstream youth—and the brands that cater to them—is this straight and honest, conservative and conscious way of thinking. Be as direct as possible—just say it like it is. If a product isn't environmentally friendly, then openly admit this and that the company takes other steps to be responsible. Create youth counsels through internships and high school work programs that become the brand's voice. The goal is to absorb that voice, and hopefully let it become a living, breathing part of your corporate culture. (Corporations looking to meet the president's challenge for volunteerism—this is a great way to start a mentoring program.)

From the BMX dirt trails in New Jersey to the climbing gyms in San Francisco, we have talked to many young consumers who discuss the issues of child or slave labor in migrant workers and overseas production as one of the things that "ticks them off." Yeah, an informed and conscious consumer is nothing new, but this youth culture will push it further than any other generation. Words like "know the source" are used to question where the product or information has come from. Case in point—whoever knew that Nike, the infallible icon of aggressive youth, would be fettered by a boycott over Vietnamese-made products?

The one thing that never goes out of style is integrity. We should start taking care of our own. I mean, basically what I try to buy is made in America—this bike is made right here. Look at what happened to Atari—gone. I try to buy American so I can keep people like my parents working.

—KEITH, NINETEEN, STUDENT,
SAN DIEGO

So the straights are more conscientious than most, but they will influence the second "green" wave of recycled, organic and responsible products. You are thinking it never really caught on—but this youth culture heading your way was weaned on recycling as a daily routine, not a chore. More than ever, they are concerned about the environment. Most volunteer youth organizations today revolve around community and land development, like building a garden in a vacant Brooklyn lot. They will support a company or product that is as environmentally concerned as they are. Among others, Ben and Jerry's ice cream made good by donating proceeds to save the rain forest.

The outdoors is being annihilated. We're trying to squeeze in as much outdoor fun as we can within the next fifteen years before there is no more wilderness left in this country. I think the outdoors will be unusable within the next fifteen years. Less wilderness to go to. Eventually it will be a giant, corded-off path with you and 400,000 other people walking around together. It's not wilderness anymore—it'll be a tour and exhibit that looks like wilderness.

—KEN, TWENTY-FOUR, PROGRAMMER/WEB DEVELOPER,
AUSTIN

But to succeed with them in the future, corporations have to move beyond a promise of monetary support (exactly to whom or what do you send money to save the rain forest anyway?). The youth we speak to are more concerned with their homeland. As more and more of them hit the hills and trails to mountain-bike, mountain-board, terrain-skate, boulder, climb and hike, they will want to know that the land will be maintained for their next adventure. Often, it's a moral code of responsibility they live by, as prevalent among climbers, alpinists and hikers. Many contribute directly, through funds and organizations like the Access Fund, which preserves the land for climbers. People with this mind-set, more than anyone, will accept the fact that someday we will have to pay to use a local park—at least it will be maintained and preserved.

Many outdoor lifestyle manufacturers support this code. To some companies, it is their philosophy. Patagonia, maker of outdoor wear, was one of the first to introduce recycled cotton T-shirts, and Burlington Denim weaved a reused denim fabric.

Using technology to recycle and create new products is another offshoot of this technorganic movement. When Wellman first came out with a fiber made from recycled plastic soda bottles, there were some nonbelievers. But the outdoor industry? They cheered the product, wearing Patagonia's polar fleece garments.

We are approaching a new millennium, and according to the underground voices, the time has come to use technology to synthetically re-create an organic experience or product. As with the technoshamanists, our need to introspect as well as connect is as much second nature as recycling. Now is the time to connect with environmentally aware and re-created products.

Politics, economics, music and fashion have cycled together since the turn of the last century—we have dressed and danced according to the political sentiments of the time. Today's street culture is no exception—"grunging down" in the early nineties and electronic-ing in the late nineties. But with all the positive mind-sets we have been discussing thus far, the trend is definitely one of gaining respect, self-control and self-promotion by cleaning up your mind, your environment, your appearance—and your body.

> I think people are gonna get scared when the whole millennium turns, they're gonna freak out, and so they're gonna return to—kind of like what I'm doing, good and wholesome—because they're scared. With the turning of the millennium it's kind of like this immediate mortality suggestion in your face. And so I think people are going to become more straitlaced as time goes on. I think there's gonna be a lot more young Republicans and I think there's gonna be a lot of religious searching.
>
> —JENNY, TWENTY-TWO, STUDENT, SAN FRANCISCO

Beyond all the fun and thinking young, the key is to have the brand really take responsibility and connect the technological advances of the business with a natural flip, to create the perfect combination of synthetic or electronic with natural elements. As one young girl expressed it recently: "I think there is nothing more magnificent than the beauty of nature coupled with the mystery of technology . . . that's truly an art form. It's like technology with a soul." Does it exist out there yet? Consider hydroponics, or the growing of plants and vegetables on water; new products from Reebok that combine breathable, natural fabrics with protective synthetics; and fashion fabrics that mix synthetics with all-natural fibers, as we discussed before. Very soon you will be greeted by the scent of grass or flowers and the sounds of wind and birds when your "sens-alarm" wakes you in the morning.

Once a product is given a technical advance, remember, give it soul and a purpose. Then, and only then, will it be *real*.

WORD FROM THE STREET

Drew Davidson, twenty-six, teacher/public speaker/working toward Ph.D. in communications, Austin, Texas.

Interviewed by Claire, Austin correspondent, in Drew's home in Austin.

Claire: How do you explain your interest in the Internet and holistic health?

Drew: I think the groups that are really into the Internet, the geek hackers, are the ones that are spearheading the resurgence in these New Age holistic healing methods and getting into tai chi, massage treatments, and meditation retreats. I think you could make an argument that it's because they spend their whole day in a cubical with a computer and they want to get out—get back in touch with their bodies, get back in touch with their selves, with their humanity—with their flesh and blood—dig back in and get dirty. You can look at computers as such cut-and-dried little places to be, if you really need to call it a place—it's sort of a misnomer, you've got the screen and that's where you start, at least right now in general. The way technology's going there's gonna be all different sorts of ways to dig into cyberspace—gloves and glasses, immerse yourself even more. They have the suit on and they come up and you see them with your little goggles and they touch you, the suit's rigged with electronic pulses so you feel the touch, electronically even though nothing touched you per se, but you see it happening and you feel it happening—so it's kind of hard to make the distinction—it's going to get better and more "real."

Claire: What's next for you?

Drew: What I'm interested in is emerging technologies and emerging theories in terms of how you take care of yourself. Looking for the fluidity—I don't think I'll ever get bored with the issues, there'll always be a better, more satisfactory way to explore things and look at things and play with things.

Andy Glickman, twenty-four, graduate student working toward master's in rhetoric, Austin, Texas.
    Interviewed by Claire, Austin correspondent, in Andy's home in Austin.

Claire: Explain the relationship between technology and spirituality people are talking about.

Andy: There is a lot of spirituality going both ways—there's a lot of people who are jumping into technology for a lot of the "salvation" that it may provide, and part of that is getting mixed in with some of the New Age and some of the older traditions. Some of the luddites who deny technology are at the same time embracing it, if for no other reason than it is with us. It is something that penetrates all of our daily lives, so one of the more interesting things is when the old and the new collide and you get interesting groups of people, like a rave is essentially a collective trance dance like the Pakistanis used to have, like the monks might have—well, the monks wouldn't dance but the same kind of thing, getting into that state, that metaphysical space—through technology, so we can actually progress a little further.

1 0

THE IMMACULATE PERCEPTION

The future will be bacteria-free germ warfare. I suspect everybody may be carrying some sort of device for a variety of survival purposes, if nothing else when the ozone gets bad. You'll see people wearing something to protect themselves from the pollution. All these things are gonna come out of L.A.; the most polluted, dirty, disgusting city on the planet will provide you with all your fashion needs for a pollution society.

—KEN, TWENTY-TWO, WEB DEVELOPER, AUSTIN

You may think that this is very far off, that germ- and pollution-barrier clothing won't be necessary in your lifetime. But if you have visited the underground club scene in London, Amsterdam or Germany anytime recently, Ken's prediction would be a reality. Gas masks, welding goggles and surgical masks are now hyped as the ultimate accessory. That and medical tops, lab coats, vomit bags—anything and everything to survive.

We as a society are fighting to save the ozone layer, voluntarily recycling to reduce pollution. Everyone talks about the environment these days, from prestigious scientists and naturalists to youth culture. Transcending fashion, barrier protection will become a necessity. Right now, consider the streets our runway to life in the septic trenches.

> I think we're all going to hell, serious. We have to change our ways, stop driving our cars and polluting. Pretty soon we'll be wearing tank suits just to breathe.
>
> —CARLOS, SIXTEEN, STUDENT, LOS ANGELES

BARRIER-TEC

Protective gear has been coming on strong in the street lines that cater to young urban trendsetters: camouflage pants, army jackets with big pockets, military-inspired backpacks, duffel bags and watches. This gear has been marketed as clothes for street survival, not the deserts or jungles. Even in young women's clothing, the move has been to cargo pants, shorts and safari jackets—again. All built around the basic premise that you need more pockets for all your "stuff."

The survival gear you see on the streets now will transform to protective gear, gear with built in blockades. Sputnik uses the term "Barrier-Tec"—technology that builds a barrier against the enemy. Barrier-Tec clothes will fight against the unseen forces of evil—germs, pollution, acid rain. It's clothing, accessories, shoes, personal products that take a cue from industries that protect their workers (or protect their products from the workers) like computer chip manufacturers, spray painting facilities, medical lab research, food processing, etc. High-tech barrier materials exist because of these industries. But what about the dirt, dust and germs in our everyday life? Why can't we have clothes made from the same materials?

So you're thinking, what could be so bad at the office or home that would make you need protective clothes? Take a look around. Whether sitting next to a computer (hopefully it's not a mainframe) or answering your cellular telephone, sucking in electromagnetic radiation is not our idea of user-friendly space. Today, there are companies designing protective uniforms coated with reflective copper particles to fight against electromagnetic radiation. The path has been set.

The street cultures have already used reflective materials and Kevlar to protect themselves from visual threats. As we said earlier, the antipollution mask is one of the most sought-after accessories on the streets, having started from cyclists and city bike messengers who wore surgical masks. Clean air—or the need to contain it—has become a fashion trend.

W&LT (Wild and Lethal Trash), a hot street line from Europe, used masks and other protective gear in its runway show. If you walked down any street in New York, London or Tokyo in the winter of 1997, you would have seen youth culture sporting protective glasses borrowed from the ski and swim sport markets. These goggles, made in rubber or plastic, had a very key purpose on the street—to keep dirt from getting into the eyes.

The need to protect will transgress from street style to our everyday apparel. In a feature in *DNR*, an apparel trade publication, undergraduates from the Fashion Institute of Technology and Parsons School of Design were asked to sketch their ideas of what we will be wearing one hundred years from now. Everyone had the same direction—totally protective and high-tech-integrated, not just fashion.

Eduardo Natal, a Parsons student, sketched for futuristic men what he called "a timeless classic black double-breasted jacket in high-tech fabric that emits a natural bug repellent" worn with a "micro-computer-chip thermal top with air filter for breathing polluted air. Top also senses internal health problems and monitors medical conditions." Lili M. Chu, a classmate, drew a form-fitting "temperature control/blood pressure/pulse sensor shirt."

Info-Tracker jacket of the future as conceived by Enyce, Inc.
Design by Omar, © 1997 Enyce.

The students' inspirations were similar to those of the hip street line Enyce, which sketched an "Info-Tracker" jacket, a Teflon-coated breathable nylon A-line swing coat with all the compulsory gadgets—like a survival pack of O_2 cartridges, dietary supplements, battery cell (for the wireless-cell-phone mike piece, microcell Pentium arm computer and virtual reality gloves), multifrequency tracking device, utility kit and first-aid kit. Oh, and a biothermal stabilizer vest for all climates.

Although we are not yet into the year 2097, fabrics and technology that protect us from extreme elements already exist, as in products from The North Face. When Conrad Anker and crew go ice climbing in Antarctica, they need gear that shields them from the subfreezing temperature and winds outside, yet keeps them dry as their bodies heat up during their climbs. Tightly woven microfiber materials laminated with Gore-Tex are breathable, windproof and waterproof; Thinsulate is warm without the bulky down filling. Pricey by most standards, these performance fabrics are already integrated into some street lines—footwear linings, gloves, hats, socks—you name it. So where will this go next? Before you leave the house, you'll slip on your temperature-controlled suit—no need for all that layering. Soon to be released: fabrics that absorb damaging ultraviolet rays. If we can have solar heat and electric cars, why not solar suits? With the fascination man has with Mars and with the idea of space stations orbiting the earth, will the streets break out an astronaut suit endorsed by NASA engineers? We know of kids searching for a full barrier-protected space-looking suit like the one featured in the 1997 Pentium chip TV commercials.

> The world is getting dirtier day by day and there's always the concept of germ warfare kicking off. Dropping stuff like that more in other places than New York City, but the threat is out there. I don't know if we'll be making germ warfare clothing, but I would definitely be willing to sport it and have it in my wardrobe just in case something goes off and I need to pull that something to protect me out of my closet.
>
> —MARK, TWENTY-TWO, HIP-HOP T-SHIRT
> DESIGNER, BROOKLYN

This race to protect is not exclusive to our exterior selves. Take the concept of Survival Tabs by Food Reserves, Inc., which are ultrahigh-calorie food tablets that provide a full dose of vitamin and mineral requirements, protein, carbohydrates, dextrose, lactose for fast energy "under desperate circumstances" and essential fatty acids for "long-lasting endurance when you need it most." In their web site posting, Survival Tabs are described as a "convenient, compact, lightweight, lifesaving food ration for any emergency." They claim to be the "Margin of Survival," that if you were lost in a jungle, you would use Survival Tabs to sustain yourself as long as necessary.

That's great for those who can't find anything to eat. But, being human, we like to chew and taste. The key here is to combine the tasty sweet fun of youth favorites like candy with antioxidant, phytonutrient supplements: things that purify the system and add minerals and vitamins to increase hearing or sight, biochemicals that are released through your pores to protect against harmful UV rays.

All our survival needs will contain nutraceuticals, phytochemicals, phytonutrients and phytofoods. Food, beverages and health and beauty products will have to contain some form of nutrient or body-enhancing formula that actually works. The Green Giant goes functional—with phytochemicals that "pump you up."

Think of how big the holistic or alternative medicine practice is becoming. By the year 2020, we will all have a holistic healer added to our list of health providers.

SURVIVAL OF THE ANTISEPTICS

Germs, the unseen enemies, plus the visible reality of pollution and environmental deterioration in street life, have prompted new concerns about the body. Sex, cleansing, bodily functions will all become preoccupations as a new paranoia about "How can I keep myself pure, clean, safe, one with my environment?" develops.

Now that the youth culture has and uses protective masks

and materials, the search is on for products that fight the unseen enemies. As Ken said (on page 152), bacteria-free germ warfare. *Sportswear International*, the surveyor of street style, dubbed it "germ war wear" in one recent issue. As the editorial feature describes it, "microbiophobia inspires antiseptic fashions for an illusion of protection against smart viruses and resistant bacteria." *Sportswear International* is right—so far. What the streets can get their hands on are clothes that give the *illusion* of protection—unless they get hold of that Intel Pentium processor suit.

The survival and protective look today is shifting to this medical twist. Street lines like Sears & Robot, A.P.C., Sada Remix and Jeremy Scott all borrow from the hospital scene for their whites, lab shirts, hypodermic needle prints, medical bags and surgical glasses. The antiseptic mood also explains the color white replacing black as the dominant street hue and the street culture's self-proclaimed shift toward "cleaning up."

Without the streets knowing it, antiseptic fashion is in the works. Burlington Denim is marketing an antimicrobial denim that keeps the dirt off and protects the skin from bacteria. Now all the alternative sports kids and outdoor enthusiasts will be able to trek in their beloved jeans.

Besides our gear, there are other hints of the antiseptic trend. Clean Call, a disposable telephone cover made by Elizabeth Wilkes of California, is meant to slip over the mouthpiece of those grungy pay phones full of flesh-eating beta strep bacteria—and who knows what else. The Tokyo Mitsubishi Bank in Japan has a new "total antigerm branch" featuring ATMs that are made in antibacterial plastic and dispense disinfected cash. The machine was developed out of the disdain many young women in Japan have for touching things handled by middle-aged men.

Being germ-phobic (microbiophobic) fuels the motive for street cultures to hunt for products that deliver; things with purpose; items that protect and shield, provide blockades from outside forces, or create the illusion that they do.

Consider Purdey's original, a sparkling herbal multivitamin fruit juice drink that is bottled in a short, completely metallic-covered (almost sterile-looking) wrap, with simple blue type (the healing color) and a metallic rip cap that has a pull like a hand grenade. It's very medicinal looking for a fruit juice drink that "tastes lively . . . clean and sparkling." Think they are on to something? It's all in the message you communicate—clean, pure, safe, herbal, vital, energy boosting, whatever. This is where the streets are heading . . . and so will we.

REACHING PURTOPIA

What we've been seeing in the past two Mindtrends reports is a vision, a utopia, of clean, holistic harmony. A haven from the stressful, polluted—physically and intellectually—dirty aspects of daily life. Wouldn't it be ideal to live sheltered from the outside world, fueling your body with Survival Tabs? Maybe not, but the word has been that simple, purer is the way to be.

> If fashion doesn't head toward functionality, it's going to fail. Seriously. I mean, realistically, the way the environment is going, we'll have to have stuff that is toxin-proof, UV-protective. You'll have to make sure your clothes don't fall off the body—we'll be wearing Kevlar suits.
>
> —BRIAN, EIGHTEEN, STUDENT/SKATEBOARDER, SAN FRANCISCO

Simplicity, to the streets, is a sign of hope lifting the anxiety that comes with the year 2000. Those thoughts have shifted to a general interest in a renewal, or what they call a renaissance.

In Austin, San Francisco and New York City, they are talking about "purifying" and a time of spirituality and oneness, a pure utopia—a "Purtopia." Purtopia, to them, is beyond making an ideal society or place—it's about achieving ideal perfection.

These new Purtopians want a society free of clutter—an antiseptic environment, enhanced by technology. Clean and simple—a place to experiment and experience new thought, in your perfect world, mind and body. A place to survive.

After World War I, Walter Gropius, the founder-director of the Bauhaus, in Germany, preached a similar belief. The Bauhaus movement conceived of environments as "machines for living," promoting pure design over decoration and decadence. This movement was one of the cradles of modernism— and the underground is returning to the Bauhaus perception of modern. Everything that surrounds you should be perceived as a machine for living.

This underground movement also embraces the Bauhaus belief in practical things and the elimination of nonessential features. Look for the return of simplicity to proliferate in the mainstream as we search for a balance between science, man and technology.

This vision of a clean, crisp ethereal future is the setting for many virtual reality environments being created in cyberspace. And, for now, this is where we can live in our own world within a world, where we have total control, and disease, decay and destruction are absent.

To say that we can paint one definitive picture of Purtopia is wrong, because reaching perfection is a subjective thing. But perhaps Purtopia will be a place where we can all start with a clean slate. Re-examine life. Question old rules. Perfection is a personal interpretation, and how we will ultimately choose or not choose to let it shape and alter our lives is our decision. But realize that the need to somehow seek personal perfection—in whatever form that may be—is a mind frame that will endure as we go into the luminescent light of the twenty-first century.

My utopia is . . . this is my utopia. Just living, just life in general. You know, I was thinking about perfection and stuff like that and if the world was perfect—and all of a sudden, it hit me. Whatever I think is perfect and whatever we think would be perfect, and what would be a perfect utopia—may really not be utopia.

—CHRISTINE, SIXTEEN, STUDENT, SAN FRANCISCO

I think we will be dressed like that movie *2001: A Space Odyssey*. Did you ever see that movie? It's a beautiful movie, the style is so beautiful. You have to watch it, because that is the style. It's so beautiful, simple and pure. I always imagine that after the millennium everybody will be walking around in white gowns saying, "Hello, hello."

—ROSALIE, TWENTY-FOUR, DESIGNER AND
STYLIST, NEW YORK CITY

11

THE COLLECTIVE VIBE . . . BRINGING THE HEADS TOGETHER

No doubt, there's a raw intellect wiring the underground street cultures, a nerve driving their social momentum and serving as their call to arms. It's not enough to understand what these cultures are about, that's just paving the street surface. Cracking their code, entering their crews is the key to future mainstream markets, as they define—and redefine—the new modernity.

And the new modernity is all about unity, the coming together in a collective thinking, a collective unity of street cultures to better their situation, seize control of their future, bringing all the creative and progressive heads together to form one collective vibe.

There is strength in numbers, and unity = numbers. Now that we understand the movements the street cultures are pushing, we need to pull out their unified thinking, extrapolate their force.

Looking back several generations, our social and political situations have traditionally influenced the ideologies of a so-called "generation." Issues like peace, freedom and individual expression have fueled our pride and motivated our protests. So have greed, success and power. The young progressive street cultures of today have all those issues to protest or demonstrate. But instead of marching united, they interconnect and unify on-line—or in their communities.

The communes of the sixties and seventies defined a peaceful, organic type of living, an existence that society deemed "counterculture."

As we've seen, communal thinking is espoused by the street cultures today, but in a more creative form that prompts advancement—of themselves and their "community," their culture. This unity thing is a very real, very strong thread that differs from past cultures. While most of us are still reeling from the corporate climbs of the eighties and the down-sizing reality check of the nineties, these cultures are collectively banding to prevent any pitfalls. When their businesses and organizations and collectives become a force to reckon with—and they will—it will be a rude awakening for the stuffed and stagnant corporate cultures that exist today.

Gone will be so-called quantitative marketing studies, which will be useless since so many consumers will be freestyling, or artificially creating their playsures and new realities, so no two individuals will make the same purchasing decisions—nor will they stop for a Netsensor (the on-line future of surveys). The big brand icons will struggle for power as DIYers invade the huge arena of mainstream business, catering to our every niche and creative whim; and as the Purtopians simplify, sterilize and streamline their existence into a world without mass products. Kiss goodbye the stale, mass-media advertising strategies as the positive anarchist Netizens hide further in their cyberworld and propel the technorganic movement that rejects the mounds of trash corporate distribution leaves behind.

What they will catapult for the new modernists and future generations coming down the pike is the collective vibe, a thinking that promotes a positive infusion of creativity, progressive thinking and independence—for one and for all. Don't be afraid, be curious. Be open-minded. Tune into their media and start digesting the personalities and influences of the new modernists.

The collective poetry community found at the Nuyorican
Poets Cafe in New York City.
Photo source: "Mindtrends" video report.

Look around and seek their influences. Visit—don't browse—their web sites, like the Future Harmonix Network, an E-zine that best sums up this collective vibe:

> Future Harmonix Network! A global Internet network of increasing the flow of communication between all individuals and collectives who are working to increase creativity, communication and community in positive ways with music and sound, technology, community celebration, ecstatic/tribal/rave dance, and/or consciousness. Half of "COMMUNITY" is "UNITY." The other half is "COMM"unication. (And ⅔ of "EVOLVE" is "LOVE"!!)

> —http://www.photon.net/harmonix/
> harmonix@photon.net

If you are not on-line today, plugged into their E-zines and web sites, then you are too late for tomorrow. Technology and the proliferation of the wired world will cause our future consumers to become more elusive as a mass, yet more accessible as a niche or target market. You'll find them hiding out in the "underwire," the extension of the underground, as they continue to seek out like-minded individuals, and form their own "tribes" and "collectives."

What they will be creating are the new *nations*. Luddites, businesses, nonbelievers will be considered "noncitizens," banned from entering a network nation. That's why we must prepare, link up, tune in and enter their wired world before it's too late.

> Tribalism may replace nationalism.
>
> Picture a world in the next century organized not around nation-states but around a new form of tribes sharing the same culture and values. It's a world where you pledge allegiance not to a republic, but to a clan.
>
> That possibility isn't too far-fetched when you take the current state of our fracturing world and overlay new information technologies and the new telecommunications infrastructure. Here's how it conceivably could play out: Digital technologies can enhance—or, depending on your perspective, exacerbate—such tendencies. They could allow people to connect with people more like themselves regardless of where they live in the world. And, ultimately, they could allow people to formally organize themselves that way.
>
> —"THE DARK SIDE" (*ON THE EDGE OF THE DIGITAL AGE*), © 1996 STAR TRIBUNE

Like the underwire cultures, the streets are also organizing, clanning and planning—even without the digital luxury of Netting. As we explained earlier, young street cultures are trying to gain their strength in numbers by forming their own groups or collectives.

> The organization I'm involved in is called One-on-One Orig-
> inal . . . an in-touch organization staying on point. You're
> head of the group, like Wu-Tang Clan. We're disciplined in
> kung fu martial arts. We're multiracial—one guy is Asian,
> and he practices one discipline, I take tai chi, and there's
> a white guy, an Indian guy, a Latino . . . the purpose is to
> stay in touch. To work together toward whatever it is you
> want to do. Right now we are looking to promote (in the
> music industry). Like Wu-Tang, you're in for life.
>
> —KEITH, TWENTY-ONE, STUDENT, ATLANTA

The Wu-Tang Clan showed young dreamers and thinkers that
as a unified force you can buck the system and control your
own future. They did it—by banding together to face the mega
record labels and empowering their creativity by saying, "It's
our way or no way." Wu-Tang wanted to record as a group and
also as separate artists, each releasing their own tracks. They
made music (and hip-hop history) as a collective with some
outstanding individual artists (like Method Man). Their way
earned them multimillion sales, an independent line of signa-

> Me, personally, I feel as if it's all about the "vibe" thing. It
> doesn't matter now what culture, what your background has
> been . . . because it's all about the future. Everything is going to
> fuse into one, since we're all part of something that's already
> been kind of separated and then come together.
>
> In the next ten to fifteen years, I definitely want to have an
> empire. When I say "I," I collectively mean a lot of people who
> have the same mind frame as I do . . . a lot of people with the
> same goals, the same sense of communal responsibility, the
> same motives, and the same morals.
>
> —BAHIA, NINETEEN, STUDENT, BROOKLYN

ture clothing called Wu Wear. This is the future, the new way of thinking individually, the collective "I."

THE REDEFINITION OF "I"

I. A noun. A funny, small letter that stands for you, the individual, the person, in the first. We've talked about individuality, but what is it really?

"Individual" has been a term used by many of the younger generation when describing their style, because they grew up on the Gap and its "individuals" advertising campaign in the eighties.

The eighties were all about selfish greed, the decade of "me," how far *I* can go, how much *I* can amass. For the new modernists of the twenty-first century, the power to progress lies in unity, and their collective "I" will become the aggressive influencing force on the mainstream. The editors of *Wired Style: Principles of English Usage in the Digital Age* refer to the collective likeness of individuals in the definition of "hive mind":

> The idea of the beehive as a collective, distributed being, a mass of 20,000 bees united into a democratic oneness. Hive mind or hive thinking or swarm behavior has been seized upon as the metaphor for digital culture.
>
> Kevin Kelly, in "Out of Control," on the Net as a hive: "The Atom is the icon of 20th century science. The Atom whirls alone, the epitome of singleness. The symbol of science for the next century is the dynamical Net. Out of it comes swarm being—distributed being—spreading the self over the entire Web so that no part can say, 'I am the I.' It is irredeemably social, unabashedly of many minds."

The "hive minds" Kevin Kelly and *Wired* magazine discuss also exist in the street cultures, as they buzz together, and

I have my own company called In Creative Unity—we put on art exhibitions, murals on the street and graphic design. (How'd you get into that?) Studied art history, graduated from UCLA in 1992 and started getting involved in ways that I could present art of my day that interested me, so I started ICU. 1992 was the year of the L.A. riots, and I thought, How could I do an exhibition that was relevant to that event? I started working with graffiti artists, spray can artists, street artists—I organized a graffiti art exhibition for the first anniversary of the L.A. riots called "An Uprising"—a good way to make a significant bite into the cultural consciousness of the U.S., of L.A. (What is the important thing to you about the art?) The important thing to me about the art is that it speaks about the concerns of our generation, and I have a big interest in politically motivated art, art that uplifts our culture, or tries to improve the society in which we live.

We have a whole generation of kids that are interested in doing artwork . . . we provide a space where we'll supply you with a canvas you can paint here in this gallery—you can have a show, go up on the Internet—and they can use their skills in a more productive way. We represent over forty artists in California, ages eighteen to twenty-seven—lots of Latinos, African-Americans, a lot of white, Asian and Filipino artists. It's a family of artists . . . for our generation, family values is groups of families, groups of people, crews of friends and family, which is like a larger family. You have, like, "tribal families"—you have five families—my friends, their families are like my family. Our generation is like the hippies of the sixties, sort of, but with a different twist. We're into family values and helping our fellow man and working toward a positive tomorrow.

—STAUCH, TWENTY-SIX, LOS ANGELES

together they swarm and spread their word. They hive in their immediate circles, like the tight alternative sports cultures—and beyond, as in their definition of "family." They view friends and their friends' families as "family."

So you are thinking, How different is this "collective I" than the core target consumer-segment groups? The difference lies in the inherent definition of this collective—beyond the tight skate, surf and alternative sports cultures; beyond the music tribes of punk, ska, hip-hop and rockabilly; beyond the cliques of high school, from the trendy and arty to the jocks. The new collective is a vibe that they tune in to, ingest as natural thinking and an ordinary value in and of itself.

You can see hints of this collective vibe in the culture today. Look at the rise of spirituality, both in the young heads and in the new market genre of New Age and self-awareness. Deepak Chopra, *The Celestine Prophecy* . . . we are all searching for that collective guidance to better ourselves. Look at the magazine *Beat Down*, a small, upstart hip-hop publication that defines itself "For the Mind and the Soul." *Beat Down* tops the credits on its masthead with this:

> The All Mighty, Most High, Creator & Judge of All Things,
> God.

A collective belief, often evident in lyrical references to spirituality, weaves through all genres of music today. In an article in *Rolling Stone* magazine, Jon Wiederhorn interviewed the alternative metal band Tool on the occasion of their new CD *Ænima*, which he calls "dense and looming." Debuting at number two on *Billboard*'s album chart in November of 1996, *Ænima*, as lead singer Maynard James Keenan says, "revolves around themes that are nearly as cleansing and life-affirming as a New Age crystal convention. It's about unity, evolution and alternative perspectives. . . . Evolution didn't stop us getting thumbs. There are a lot of metaphysical, spiritual and emotional changes going on right now, and we're just trying to reflect that."

In our "Mindtrends" biannual video trend report, we have

documented progressive heads referencing Buddhism and a general belief in reaching a higher karma. These individuals are trying to achieve this structurally. Feng shui, "wind and water," is a Chinese "science" based on the ancient teachings of "chi"— the flow and quality of energy. "Chi" is considered a natural part of the universe and affects each individual differently based on their home and work environment. Today, it is practiced as a means to increase positive energy and to open a path to the enhancement of one's quality of life. This is achieved by changing the flow or structure of the home or work environment.

Eastern philosophy, because of its encouragement of mind-expanding experiences, is accepted as another extension of individual spiritual belief. The art of Zen meditation and the philosophies of the martial arts are other prevalent forms of inner expression for the progressive street cultures.

Personal religious belief has been a deep yet public issue among the hip-hop crowd and African-American culture as a whole. Athletes, artists and movie stars have publicly given first and foremost thanks to God in virtually every open acceptance or recognition of their achievements. They are giving props, due respect to the most high that empowered and blessed them to become the beings they are. Look at any credit listing on their CDs, their lyrics—and their emerging music genres, as gospel becomes hip again.

This spiritual recognition is also manifested in alternative club cultures that artificially create a spiritual environment in the form of a rave or underground dance party. Like the technoshamanists we discussed, the collective dance is often referred to by every participant as a spiritual experience.

The Moon Tribe is another spiritual gathering based around the cycles of the moon. Known to draw anywhere from five hundred to five thousand individuals, the Moon Tribe occurs once a month in the deserts of California.

Music is a collective thread in all youth cultures. The techno

(Where is the underground scene going?) In Southern California it's moving away from the warehouses and L.A. and it's all being moved out to the desert—and now the Bureau of Land Management is planning to stop all parties that are thrown out there—we have nowhere else to go, and there's thousands of people that are into this music, the harmony.

There's this thing called Moon Tribe that happens every full moon, no matter if it's on a weekend or on a weeknight, like tomorrow night. Bunch of people that get together every month to witness a full moon and listen to the best music—unlike a party where people sort of pass out, this is something that makes people look at their lives in the right way. (This happens in different places?) Yeah, in the desert, in really beautiful areas. (How many people are at these parties?) Well, tomorrow night's Moon Tribe might get up to at least two hundred people—but then, sometimes you might get up to five thousand people. They're all kinds of people—black, white, yellow, green (laughs). Really, I've been to a party in San Diego about two years ago and there must have been at least twelve thousand people.

—ERIN, TWENTY, DJ, LOS ANGELES

movement, the morphing of various sounds and familiar rhythms to create a fast, fluid, trancelike beat is an example of a uniquely underground movement surfacing into the mainstream. If you stop any average teenager or young adult today and ask them what kind of music they listen to, the answer most likely will be *everything*, from hip-hop to jazz to rock to classical. Music as the definer of tribes and subcultures is moving into a collective groove, and the new music genres today are pushing it further. Techno as a mass pop-culture music genre hasn't peaked yet, it's only just begun its pitch. But what happens when everything has a "techno" slant or tone to it, like what has happened to the "category" of alternative rock? It crashes, burns out, as the truly cool move on to the next form. What will be next? It's brewing now, in the form of more intellectual lyrics that offer compelling messages about the collective vibe.

Even Dr. Dre, the once notorious gangsta rapper noted as one of the influential innovators of hardcore rap, took a new spin when he left Death Row Records and started his own label called Aftermath. The introductory CD cover pictured the explosion of a bomb (possibly the big one), and the compilation's first song featured an East and West Coast unity rap with Nas, KRS-One and Be-Real of Cypress Hill. This happened in the wake of the rappers Tupac (2Pac) Shakur's and the Notorious B.I.G.'s deaths. There is a belief that the war between East and West has come to an end. (In the mid-nineties heyday of hip-hop, there emerged a perceived battle between the coasts, as both grew rich with their distinctly different styles and lyrics that disrespected one another.) Dr. Dre also contributed to this breakthrough compilation with "Been There, Done That," in which he closes the chapter on his hardcore style and introduces his positive-minded messages.

> The year 2000—the millennium—we have to bring it all together. It's all in unity, you know, we come together—it's nothing but power. United as one, peace we're representing.
>
> —TONY, SEVENTEEN, STUDENT, LOS ANGELES

Not every city has a ghetto, nor has all of youth culture ever visited one. But the ghetto exists as a metaphor in the lyrics of many rap artists, a metaphor for the conditions in society today, and the conditions facing them in the new millennium. The ghetto symbolizes strife, poverty, racism and disparity. This is a collective consciousness uncovered when we asked more than 420 progressive individuals aged sixteen to twenty-nine, in eight major cities across the country, what they thought the year 2000 would be like. The number one response was that they believed in Armageddon (the scene of the battle between the forces of good and evil foretold in the New Testament). They are not talking about a full-fledged war here—their view of Armageddon is the emergence of a new world order. They predict that the old-guard way of politics and business will fold to the multicultural, independent new guard who will create this new world order. This thinking is referenced in the lyrics of hip-hop, R&B and progressive rock today. It's the reason why heads are collectively clanning and creating independent organizations. It will be mainstream America's wake-up call.

THE NEW ORDER

It's all about empowerment: the new thinkers coming into their own power, infiltrating the old-guard businesses and old-guard politics and changing the order. It's not a black versus white, Asian versus Hispanic thing; it's about coming together as a new order to make a difference.

> The year 2000 is coming and everyone must prepare, but I don't think people know what they're preparing for. So much transition going on, it's creating this global energy—I tend to be pessimistic to the planet and mankind. A lot of people are complacent and don't try to change things. I see technology advancement as a breakdown in human communications, so I'm scared.
>
> I have a personal obligation to better society, to better humankind, but I don't know how to do it, so it's become frustrating. Hopefully people will become empowered and make a difference—more of what a tribal community is all about.
>
> —SARAH, TWENTY-ONE, STUDENT, SAN FRANCISCO

This collective thinking will fuel a call to self-empowerment. Empowerment isn't a militant thing—what the streets are driving is of the mind. Members of street cultures are using the mind, not just emotions, arming themselves with the knowledge to start a business, to spread a message through music or a zine, and to run for office.

Earlier generations were taught to go to school, to get ahead, to climb the corporate ladder, to be respectable members of society. These young cultures aren't being taught—they are *learning* how to survive. How to be street-smart.

East New York's rapper Jeru the Damaja is a modern-day prophet who, through his lyrics, is educating hip-hop culture on the power of intellect and the mind. Embedding biblical imagery and philosophies of the Muslim Five Percent Nation sect in his lyrics, Jeru rhymes about the evils of greed, lust and materialism and warns of the near reality of Armageddon.

Excerpts from an interview with Jeru the Damaja by Mary McGuinness, in the December 1996 issue of *Sportswear International*:

MIND OVER MATTER

He won't don gold chains, Versace or Armani and he doesn't sip Moet & Chandon. He's the self-proclaimed messiah of hip-hop and preaching knowledge, and understanding is his style.

It's no secret that hip-hop is in a crossfire. In an attempt to expose the "black experience" it has fallen victim to its commercialism. What started as an ingenious enterprise—local B-boys spinning and scratching wax at block parties while MCs improvised rhymes over beats—has become transformed into a musical genre that celebrates "Versace," "Tommy," "DKNY," "kilos," "Moet" and "gats." But, according to kung-fu-suited rapper Jeru the Damaja—this is all about to change.

Armed with the beats of master conductor DJ Premier, the militant will of Malcolm X, the spiritual conviction of an oppressed preacher, and the full-proof strategy of a mathematician—East New York's Jeru, born Kendrick Davis, is out to rhythmically reeducate the hip-hop culture with his sophomore album *Wrath of Math.* His quest is to enlighten his message-free contemporaries (musical artist Foxy Brown for example) and the world—of what he feels has been forgotten: The positive power of hip-hop.

Chillin' on Payday Records' vintage sofa in baggy blues, a nondescript pullover and an Afrocentric knit cap (he says his hair is too powerful to witness)—Jeru begins to explain how hip-hop has been taken hostage by materialism and violence (personified in his song "One Day") and how this Soldier for Culture intends to free hip hop from its "invisible chains."

MARY: How would you define hip-hop culture today?

JERU: It's the life in the inner city . . . Hip-hop is the sole voice of the youth movement, because we really don't have any other voice. You get into basketball, you really don't get to say that much—every other sport, you just get to use your body.

MARY: Why are you so outspoken about material worship on your album?

JERU: Just because something is happening doesn't mean it's right. There were slaves, that don't mean it was right. So if you're bragging about how much money you have, really show me. Don't show me your car, I could have five of those cars. Buying cars, $200 bottles of champagne and all that, it's destructive. Show me something constructive . . . like fixing up the community or making black distribution companies.

MARY: But why do you think the hip-hop community has embraced haute-couture brands—designers that don't even target the African-American market?

JERU: It's gonna change. You're still gonna have people that do it, but it's not always going to be like that. People are going to wise up one day, and by that time, they probably will have made so much money off them that it won't matter. It's a fad. Before Versace, it was Gucci and Louis Vuitton.

MARY: What would you say to Calvin Klein or Versace if you could confront them face-to-face?

JERU: Nothing. No message for Calvin. Versace—none of them. They know what they're doing. I'm gonna walk up to Klein and say, "Hey, you're exploiting the black underclass," and he's gonna say, "Yeah, alright . . . so?"

MARY: So is social awareness the driving force behind your music?

JERU: My driving force is life, living. Nothing more. Nothing less.

MARY: In your lyrics there is a lot of biblical imagery. There's your song "Life of a Prophet," and on Disc Two, your spoken word piece, you refer to the Apocalypse. Is your belief in God a reason that you're hell-bent on denouncing material worship?

JERU: God? I'm God.

MARY: You're God? Seriously?

JERU: I'm God. Don't you know that the black man is God. That's the oldest thing in the world.

MARY: Do you believe in a higher power than yourself though?

JERU: A higher power than the mind? The higher power is the mind. The mind created everything in front of your face. The mind is more powerful than anything.

MARY: So do you think people should worship you?

JERU: No. Worship yourself. Because there is no such thing as heaven and hell. Everything in the universe is 360 degrees—it's all mathematics. And the original mathematics is sound. That's why they say in the beginning there was a Big

Bang. That's why they call you a person . . . "persona" means through sound. It's not chance or luck or the will of a mystery god. It's mathematics and effect.

MARY: Are you the reactor?

JERU: I'll bring the reaction full fury.

MARY: So if everything is scientific to you, why do you preach lyrics like "You fools, you work all week and give the devil back his loot for jewels" on the song "Ya Playin' Yaself."

JERU: Because science is knowledge. And knowledge, wisdom and understanding is the true key to wealth. Yet the Bible tells you that knowledge and understanding is the way to find out about God. In the Bible, the 82nd Psalm and St. John chapter 10, Jesus tells us that we are all gods, and that's way the church hated him. Because if the church can have you confused about the biggest question in life—and that's God—it will always be a mystery to you, so . . . what will you ever really know? That's the secret of God. Therefore the secret to knowledge. I'm God . . . we are all Gods in our own right. Everything came from God, and that means everything is God, and I'm the being that can project God the most powerful and efficient, because I am the image and likeness of God. This is not a belief. It is knowledge.

MARY: Do you think people—designers—are going to be scared of your message?

JERU: If you're afraid of it then you're probably the enemy.

MARY: When you speak of the Apocalypse are you referring to the death of today's hip-hop—violated by violence and material worship—or the end of time?

JERU: Apocalypse will come when I stop making records. And then, people are going to be fighting over a copy at the end of the world, so they can learn how to live. And when it comes down to it, you're not going to care about what you've got on. Your life is on the line—it's going to be what's in your head that counts.

MARY: Not money?

JERU: In this society you only need money to live. That's one

> of the traps they put on you to try and stop God from being God—you become slave to a dollar bill.
>
> MARY: How do you know your message of positive intelligence is going to change anything?
>
> JERU: Every time you say something, you're changing something. I say what I say because I know that's the truth.

If you think that this new order belief is one that is skewed by age, ethnic or urban origin, think again—62 percent of the people who believed in Armageddon were between the ages of sixteen and twenty-two and of diverse ethnicities.

The other most common answer to what they believed the year 2000 would bring was that America will be like the 1930s socially and politically. The 1930s marked the end of the Great Depression, when Roosevelt emerged as the new hero with his socialist New Deal program. The collective vibe will bring a New Order Deal to corporate America—a freestyle thinker in every cubicle and a virtual or DIY niche business under every corporate umbrella. Collective thinkers will start training the generations following them, empowering them with the knowledge to succeed. Like the telephone, the Internet will become our daily form of communication, and the linkage, the hiving of collective thinkers will form orders stronger than the political and social organizations that exist today.

We all know that the formation of a third political party is not far . . . but what will happen when the collective thinkers decide they don't want to vote—that they want to drop out? Or empower themselves? Or create their own cooperatives, collective living and shopping quarters? Or they may live and exist among the mainstream, but support the new "independents," the new cooperatives. The challenges for manufacturers will not be what products to create and market, but how to have a megabrand embraced by these future consumers.

Think about it . . . manufacturers will have to include community and street distributors under their corporate structure, extending the network of distribution to actually *be local*.

Clothing manufacturers will face a challenge as consumers walk away from "being someone's walking billboard" and embrace clothing made by their own. Case in point—Enyce, a casual-streetwear line (backed by Fila, the sports conglomerate) whose management and design team are hip young individuals who put Mecca USA, a successful startup streetwear line in the early nineties, on the map. Under the influence of music and community roots, Enyce has a corporate mind-set of creating "universal wear," because, according to Tony Shellman, Enyce's creative visionary, the heads "are growing up, taking charge, making a difference" in society and their lives . . . the ultimate collective-vibe wear. Perhaps Fila understood that financially backing individuals with the respect and knowledge of the streets will keep them on a trend in a volatile marketplace.

What the new order will also bring is a new creative empowerment. We've gone through a turbulent decade in the nineties—government reduced funding for the arts, and the streets had to seize the moment. Beyond the creativity in their music, we witnessed the return of graffiti art as self-expression. Messages from the street hit the galleries, soft-drink cans, T-shirt designs, wallpaper and book covers.

The hunger for creative expression thrives in this youth culture, and the new collectives base some of their needs on creative empowerment. Like the One-on-One Originals in Atlanta (see page 166), there are creative writing groups, independent film production groups, video production groups, design coalitions, and so on, all surviving in a society of big business.

Don't think this collective vibe thing is too esoteric for big

"Keeping' da shit zureal" shares the unity.
T-shirt by Zulu Sky.
Photo source: "Mindtrends" video report.

business—it's here, and it's a viable thing. MCI, in their introduction of a new Internet service, used the collective vibe mentality in a national TV campaign that explained to all nonbeliev-

> There's no place like the Point (Hunt's Point, Brooklyn) in that we are so artistically inclined, as well as educationally. We let the kids know that they can express themselves through poetry, that they can express themselves through dance and physical movement . . . and that's really what this place is all about, as well as thinking business-minded. Because they have to learn how to make money and survive in this world. We have the Business Incubator here . . . we have the kids with the ideas and energy, and we give them guidance and polish it up so that they can do something really concrete with that. They can rent the incubator space out for very cheap—learn about the business there and then move out into the mainstream.
>
> —CARIDAD, TWENTY-THREE, STUDENT, BROOKLYN

ers that on the Net there is no color, no age, no infirmities—that everyone is connected equally. The tag line for the MCI TV campaign really sums up the street's outlook on this intellectual union they are spreading: "Is this a great time or what?"

Even cookie-cutter retailer the Gap recognized that everyone is truly an individual, featuring rapper LL Cool J in a TV commercial wearing a Fubu-brand hat (what, no Gap?). They went so far as to recognize that other brands do exist, and that we don't all have to be Gapped out from head to toe. Props to LL Cool J for his poem about universal unity even though it spells out "Gap."

The message of a collective unity is one that will proliferate in the coming years, as the achievers of today train the next generation, challenging the traditions and establishments we hold true today: What is power? What is rich? What is poor? What is masculine? What is feminine? With these questions comes possibility, because here come the freestylers, DIYing their artificial playsures, spreading their message of positive anarchy and driving toward Purtopia—all as a means of survival in this new century of change.

Do you know what connects us all? On the Net it's called PLUR. No, it's not a dishwasher detergent, it's an acronym that stands for Peace, Love, Unity and Respect. These are big words and may be difficult to define but here are some ideas:

Peace: The calmness you find with those around you, and also inside of yourself. It's tough, we often have to work at it but when you're at peace with others, with ourselves and with our planet, only good can come of it.

Love: The caring you feel for friends, for strangers, for those in need and also for caring you show for yourself. It's symbiotic, it's about sharing—whatever energy you put into something will be returned to you!

Unity: This means we all share a lot of common things, regardless of our age, gender, race, orientation, whatevah! We are all human beings, we all need other people, and we're all in this for the happiness experienced by being around others. Though we may have differences, we all arise from the same source.

Respect: This may mean respect for others, their ideas, their music and their lives. It's also respect for one's self; one's body and the needs that it has (food, sleep). Educating yourself on the substances you ingest shows love and respect for your body; passing on the knowledge to others shows respect and love for your fellow person. :)

—A LITTLE SOMETHING DJ SPOOKY, A FAMOUS UNDERGROUND DJ IN THE AMBIENT AND ILLBIENT MOVEMENTS, WROTE WITH A FRIEND TO HAND OUT AT THE PARTIES THEY SPIN

WORD FROM THE STREET

Eric, twenty-three, fine artist, New York City
  Interviewed by Sushi, Sputnik's New York City correspondent, in Eric's home in Manhattan.

Sushi: What do you like to do in your free time?

Eric: I really like reading old books—really old books, like Mark Twain and Oscar Wilde—because I think that what people were feeling a hundred years ago is a simple kind of intellect that inspires me, that I feel like I would not want to lose in our society today which could be a little bit more complicated with this high-tech media. I mean, I have a computer so I could feel like I'm in this century—which I am—so it's interesting to me. But I really get much more inspired by raw intellect.

Sushi: What do you think the future has in store for us?

Eric: I think if anything, right now we're learning to unveil depression that was predominant within the past few centuries—and I think the next millennium is going to bring us an unveiling of feelings to allow us to stay in touch with ourselves more because that's the only way we're going to be able to evolve—by getting in touch with our feelings through sensitivity. And I feel there's a lack of sensitivity and unfortunate jadedness that has been predominant in the last few years. I see the next millennium as a good change because I think there's going to be some sort of enlightenment—by looking within ourselves and being more sensitive to others' feelings.

Sushi: What's exciting?

Eric: Basically, I think what's new and exciting right now hasn't arrived yet and I feel it's going to arrive in the next few years. I think people are feeling pressure. I think the millennium is a good excuse to create new things, which is wonderful because it keeps the human race interesting—but I think it's going to be simplified, and people are going to realize that you can do a whole lot more with less.

Sushi: What do you see for the future?

Eric: I don't see that there's going to be any major peace thing that is going to be happening in the near future—but I do think that people are beginning to learn by our minds developing into a more spiritual awareness, which is part of our natural evolution—that prejudice does hurt and that we don't like hurt.

12

THE STREETS ON THIS THING CALLED TOMORROW

I see the future as the youth getting smarter, more intelligent. We should try to unify, that's what I hope can happen in the future. But we're still killing each other, it's no different than slavery. We're enslaving ourselves mentally, physically and spiritually. But for the future, I do see a change if we can unify and try to generate the money together as a family—that's what I hope in the year 2000.

—IMANI, SIXTEEN, STUDENT, LOS ANGELES

Future won't be George Jetson kind of future that people envisioned fifteen years ago . . . it will look pretty much like it does now.

—CHRIS, TWENTY-THREE, STUDENT, PORTLAND, OREGON

I think the future will look like this—take a video and hit the fast-forward-search button. Everything is getting faster—people don't have time to stop and look around them.

—TAMARA, SIXTEEN, STUDENT, PORTLAND, OREGON

The future is the scariest thing to me . . . the future is now.

—JENNY, TWENTY, STUDENT, SAN FRANCISCO

The distant future—it's kind of scary, but I imagine the future as a scene out of *The Terminator*, where there's people versus people. I think the street people are going to continue and grow, and I think the more sophisticated people are going to stay indoors. I think there is going to be a major separation between the two.

—ATTUSA, TWENTY-FOUR, STUDENT, LOS ANGELES

In the future, everything will be back like it used to be with the earth like a garden, just because that's where real happiness is and peace—in nature. And we're so far from that right now . . . everything is so industrial.

—JADE, TWENTY-TWO, STUDENT, LOS ANGELES

Oh, the future is all about computers and new media, but I think the real new media is probably person to person or better communication. That's more valuable than the Internet will ever be. Yeah, because if everything lost power, where would we be? Talking, just like we are in this room.

—MYLES, TWENTY-ONE, STUDENT, SAN DIEGO

2010? 2020? I think it's just gonna be faster communication—faster than it is now. Still don't see governments changing that much to do great causes. This whole capitalistic greed will still be around—people will be killing each other for money, wherever it is. The U.S. might not be the U.S. anymore—might not have as much power in the world as we do now. 2020 . . . it's hard to say because I think other countries are definitely coming up with economic power—the Asian block, the European block—it's gonna be interesting who's gonna be making global influences then.

—LEE, TWENTY-ONE, WEB SITE DESIGNER, AUSTIN

The future? I think of this writer Aldous Huxley, who wrote the book *Brave New World*. Basically, the philosophy of the book is "What we love will kill us," which is very profound. Because we surround ourselves with all these things, these icons or these status symbols, which for some reason, we're thinking that we need to be here (holds her hand up high), when we can't even afford to get there. We don't even consider the steps in between, so the future looks very grim.

—MAESHAY, TWENTY-ONE, STUDENT, NEW YORK CITY

We'll be running around on hoverboards—won't even need skates or wheels, we'll just be floating around.

—JAKE, SEVENTEEN, STUDENT, SAN DIEGO

I think technology is here to stay, but I can't imagine that it can be trendy forever. People might be staying indoors more, having New Year's over the Internet. We may become conscious of it and not be so into technology. Think young people are becoming more politically aware, thinking ahead about the environment and global and social issues. Hope politics of this country are not going to keep polarizing and get way out of control and revolutionary—it's a really frightening thought.

—JUSTINE, TWENTY-SIX, GRADUATE STUDENT, AUSTIN

People are going to be totally wired—like a whole personal computer. For real—we'll have built-in phones, computer chips under our skin, watches built in our wrists . . . it's gonna be crazy.

—LISAND, TWENTY-FOUR, DESIGNER, SAN FRANCISCO

The future, to me, looks hopeful. It looks powder blue with a little bit of pink sprinkled on. It will look like this (shows fantasy globe) . . . that's the future. I see a bubble of happiness and I see prettyism.

—RICHIE RICH, TWENTY-FIVE, ANDROGYNOUS POP
SINGER/PERSONALITY, NEW YORK CITY

AFTERWORD:
HOW TO HEAD-HUNT, NOT COOL-HUNT

What's cool? That's a question that makes ratings rise. Corporate America smile. Sputnik correspondents cringe—and the fringe run. The word *cool* has become the hot media buzzword. And like the terms *extreme, alternative,* and *urban, cool* has made its way into every youth culture story.

As long as the underground is misinterpreted, labeled and packaged by the press, then elusive they will remain. On this current quest for *cool,* Sputnik has been deemed "cool-hunters" by the media. If you still perceive us as this after reading this book, then you have missed the big picture. What's cool? Who's cool? *Who cares?* These are the wrong questions. Going into the communities with a "cool" agenda will get you nothing but glazed stares and "I don't know" answers.

The Sputnik network is about what's real. What's happening right now in the present lives of extremely influential progressive cultures. If you take the time to understand their present, you can look to the future and interpret lasting trends that will alter and shape mainstream youth markets.

What are young people thinking? Where are their heads at? These questions are the starting point. It's not a visual thing. If you strictly "cool-hunt" then you won't understand *why:* why street cultures are dressing eighties but thinking things about unity that smack of the sixties. The trouble with hunting for cool is that it leaves you with an exterior picture that lacks meaning and content. The challenge to those who want to seek and write the truth is how to get inside the head. To be welcomed, to have a mutual dialogue.

The cool hunt then becomes the "head hunt." Cool-hunters become head-hunters, and out of this comes a basic rule the Sputnik network lives by—to quote Edward R. Murrow, "content always over the packaging."

LEARN TO EDIT

The strongest attribute a Sputnik correspondent can have is their ability to edit—to get past the facade and get inside the head to uncover the trend. This ability to sort through conventional stereotypes will become mandatory as street cultures become more connected than ever before.

There is a fusion happening on the streets. Diverse cultures are borrowing and mixing influences from one another. It is happening in the music, the fashion and in the venues where they congregate. Distinct classifications can no longer be made when it comes to this young consumer.

These new consumers have learned to edit. To cut through the clutter and find the content that speaks to them personally.

This is the challenge for marketers as we move closer to the millennium. The rapid flow of ideas, the changing street scenes, the fusion of cultures can create confusion. Trying to find the big idea has become more complex. Entering from the right avenue to get to this young consumer has become a challenge. The solution, once again—learn to edit. Learn to listen and sift through the excitement and energy of what this young consumer is saying—get to the content. There is always a unifying theme, a consistent point of view that spreads throughout youth cultures.

These consistent themes make up "Mindtrends." They are the themes that keep cutting through the clutter. Themes that touch the consumer *personally*. They are themes that carry the content that has a long-term effect on street cultures. They are the "mindtrends" that Sputnik will continue to track in the coming years because they are the trends that will last and evolve into tomorrow.

Page numbers of photos appear in italics.

JANINE LOPIANO-MISDOM (right) and JOANNE DE LUCA (left) are the cofounders of Sputnik. Through Mindtrends, their biannual trend report, they track the movements emerging among progressive youths and interpret them into actionable opportunities for marketing, new product development, brand management and advertising.